I0502608

Enjoy Mandala Coloring

Copyright: Published in the United States by Christopher Bollinger
Published January 2017
ISBN-13: 978-1542679909
ISBN-10: 1542679907

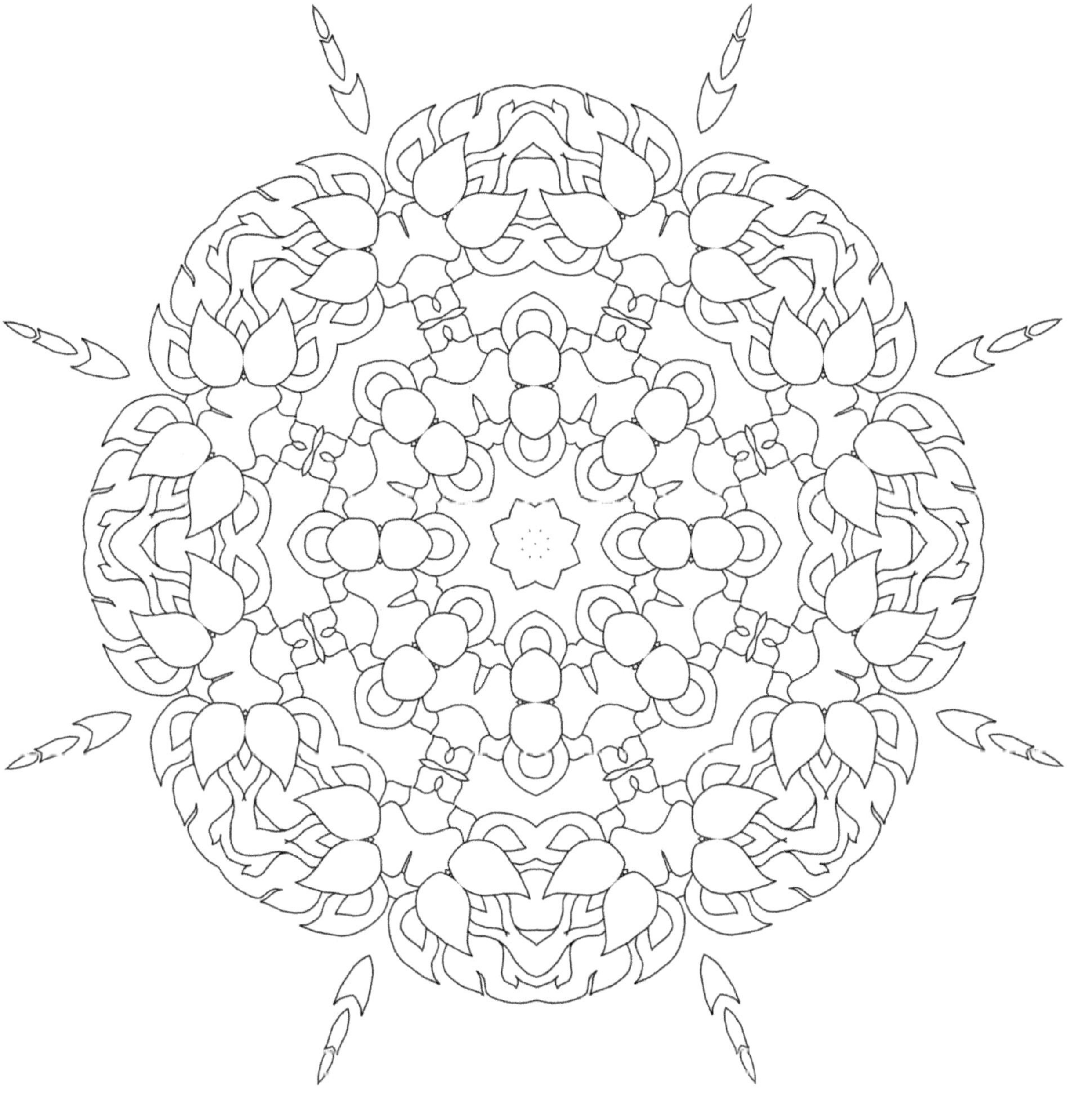

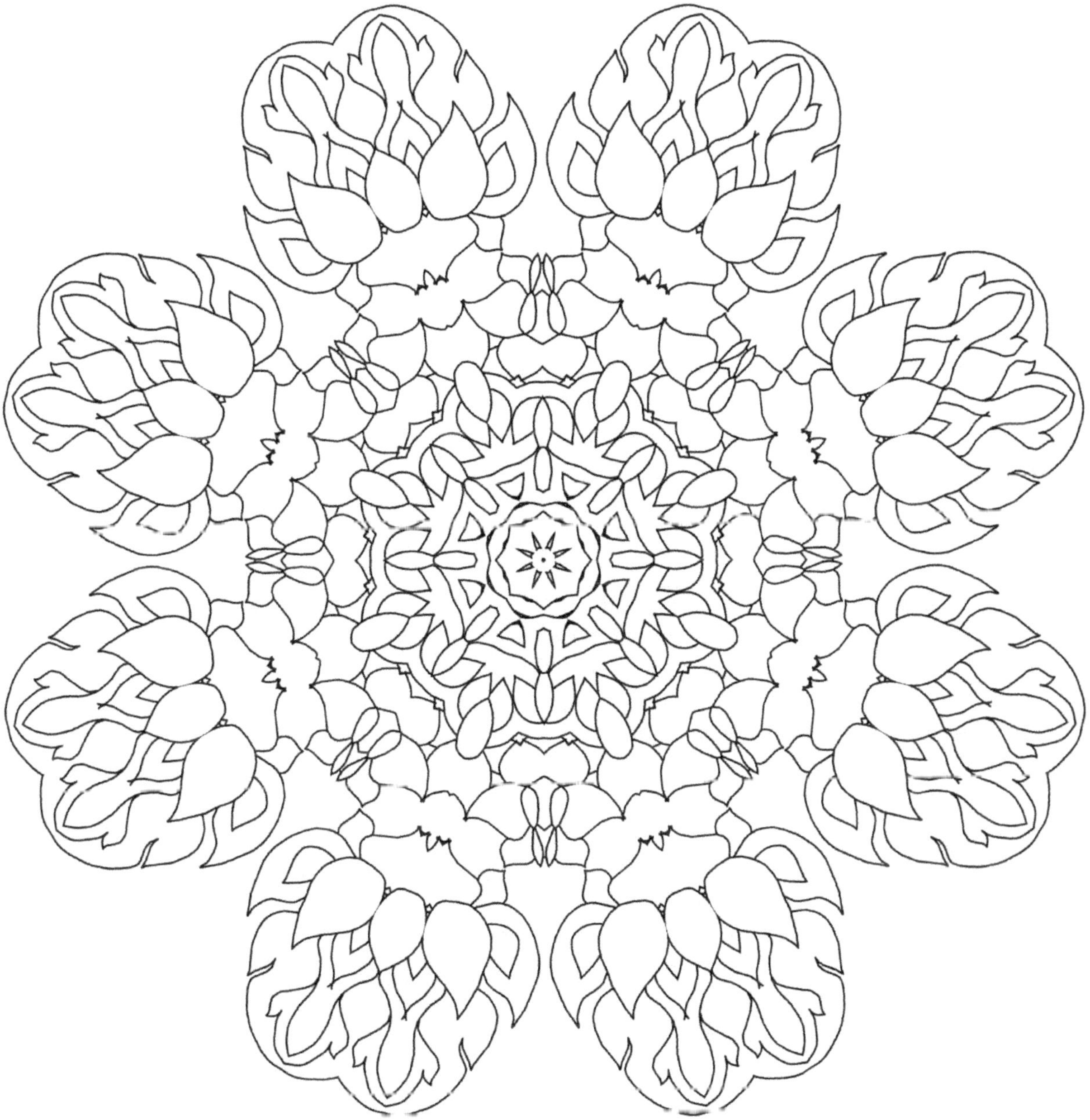

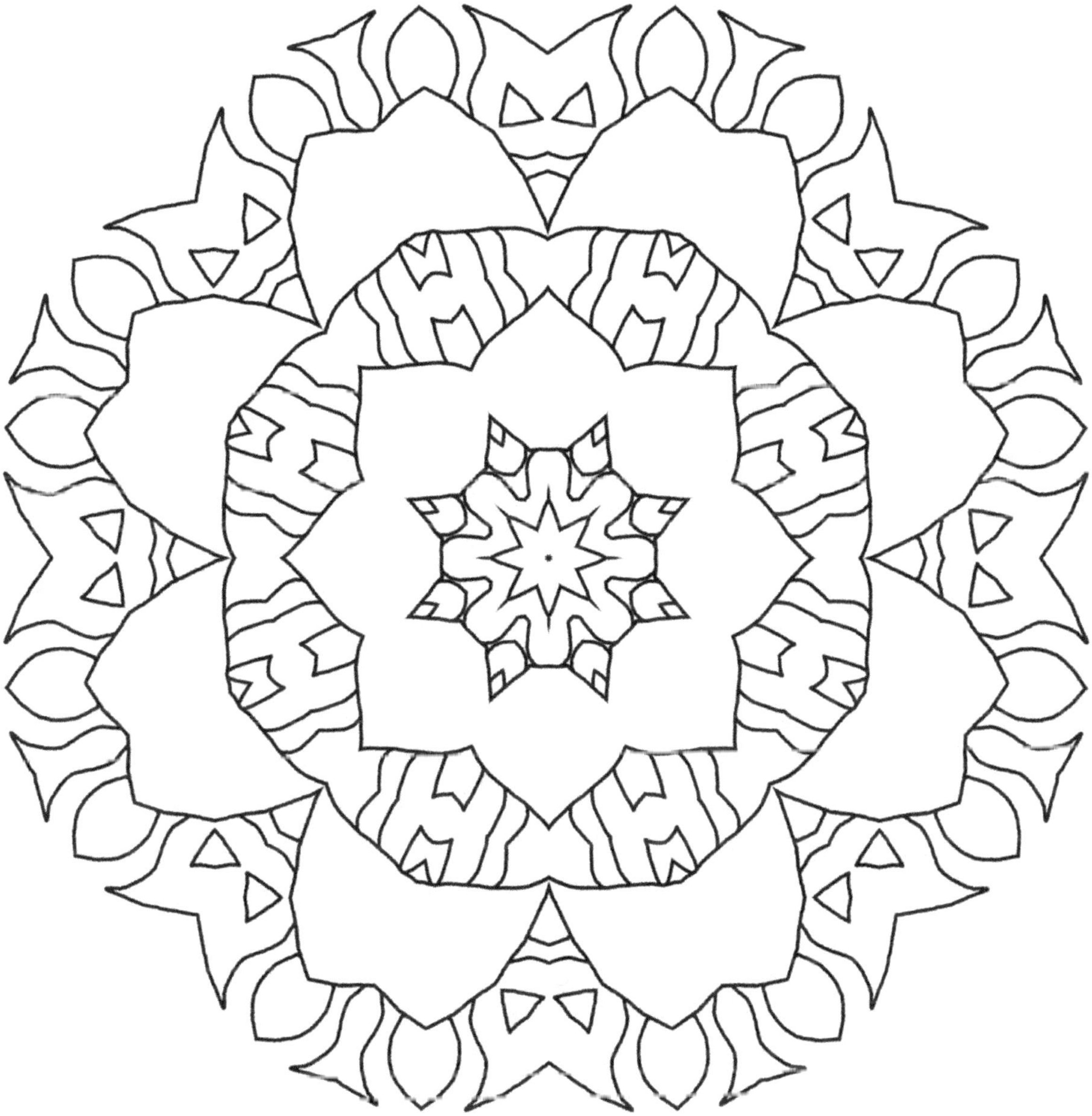

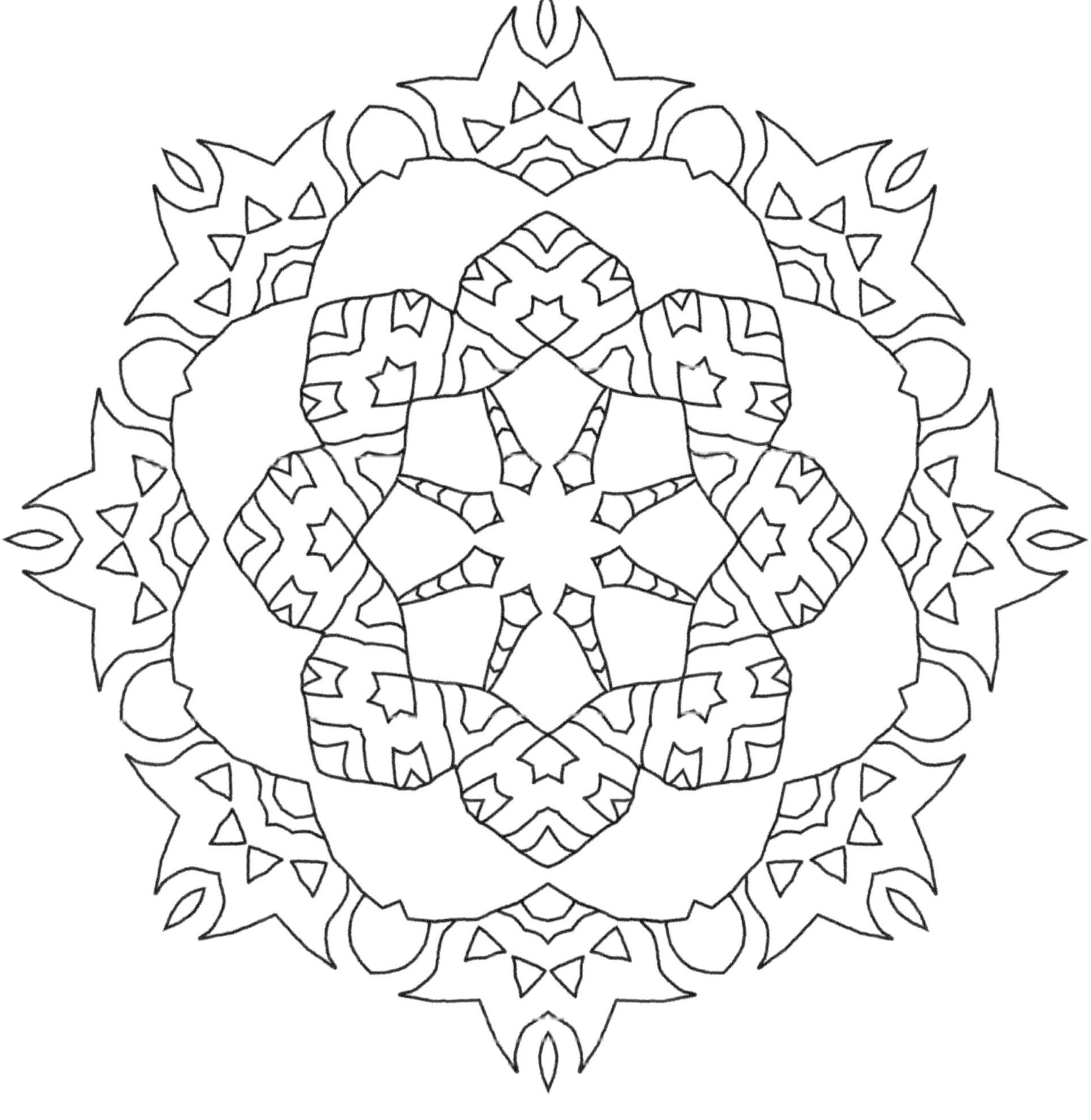

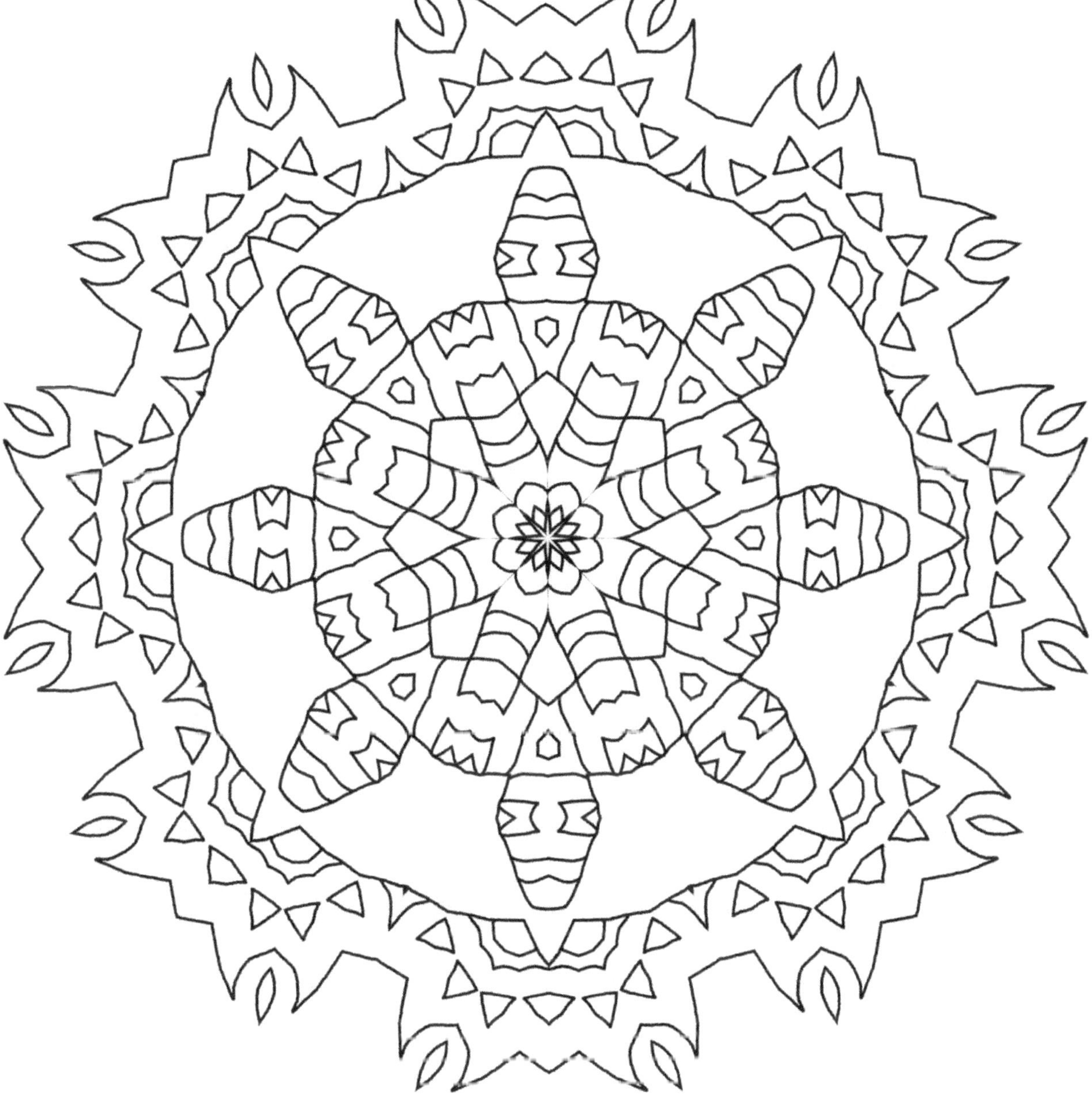

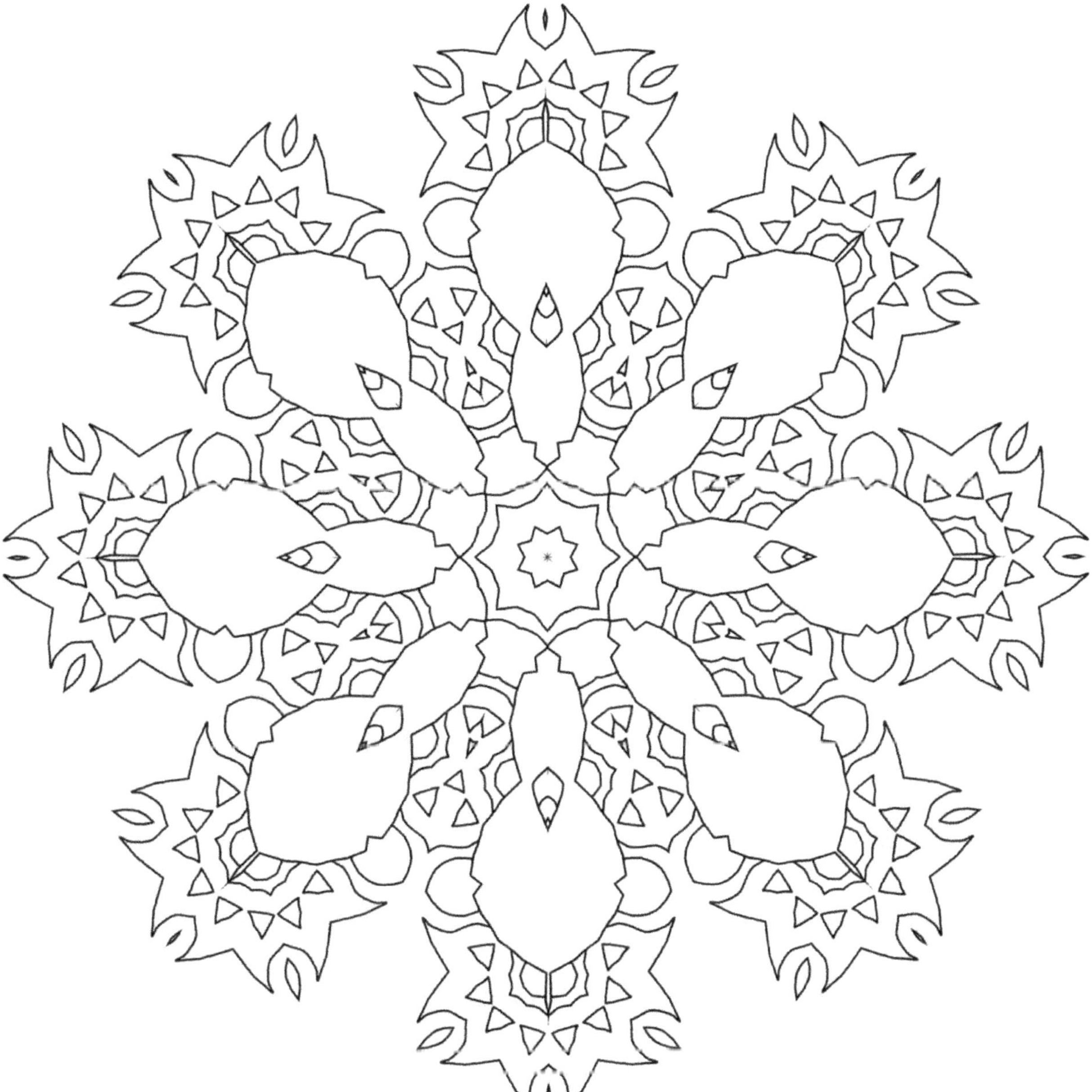

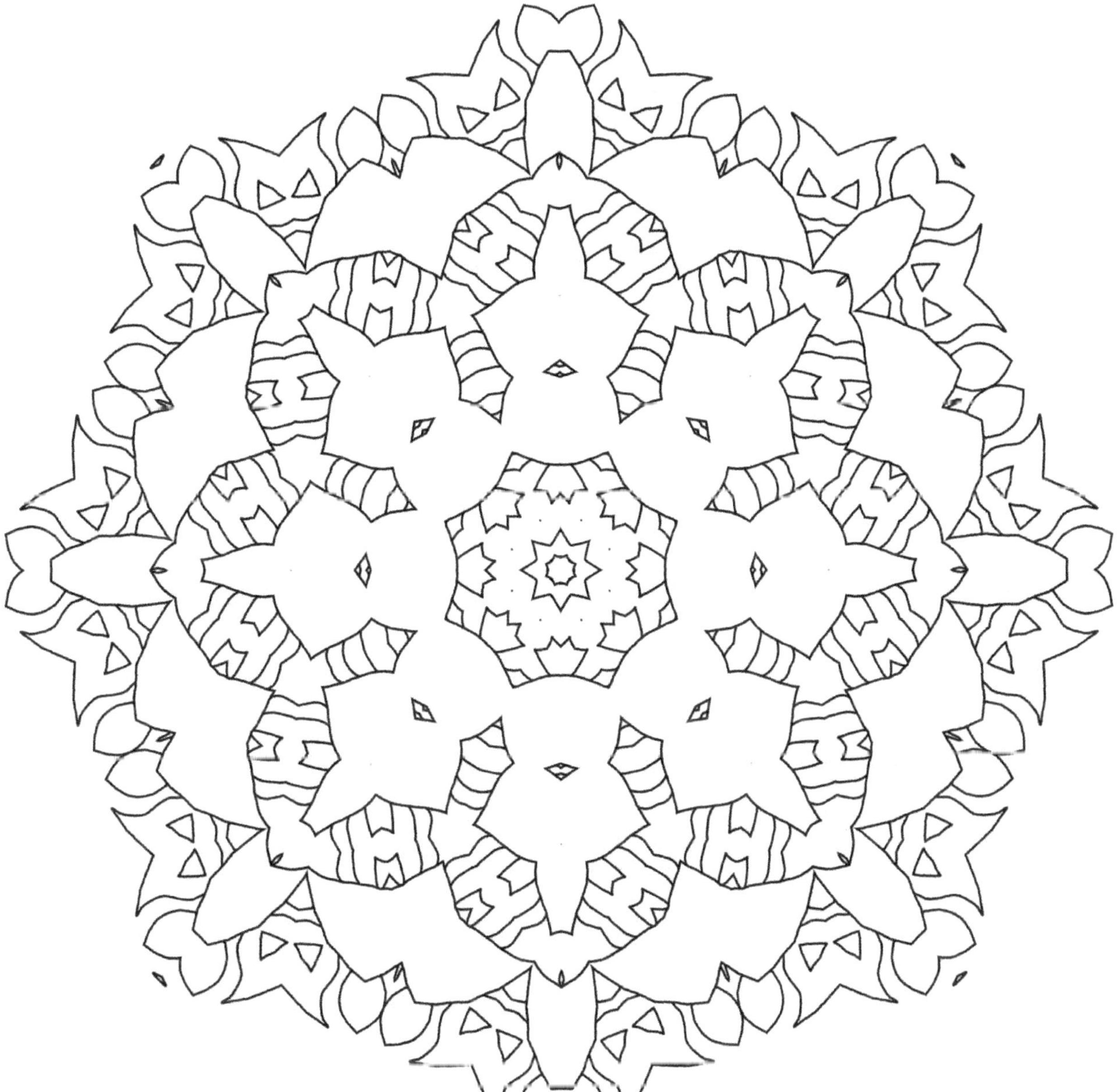

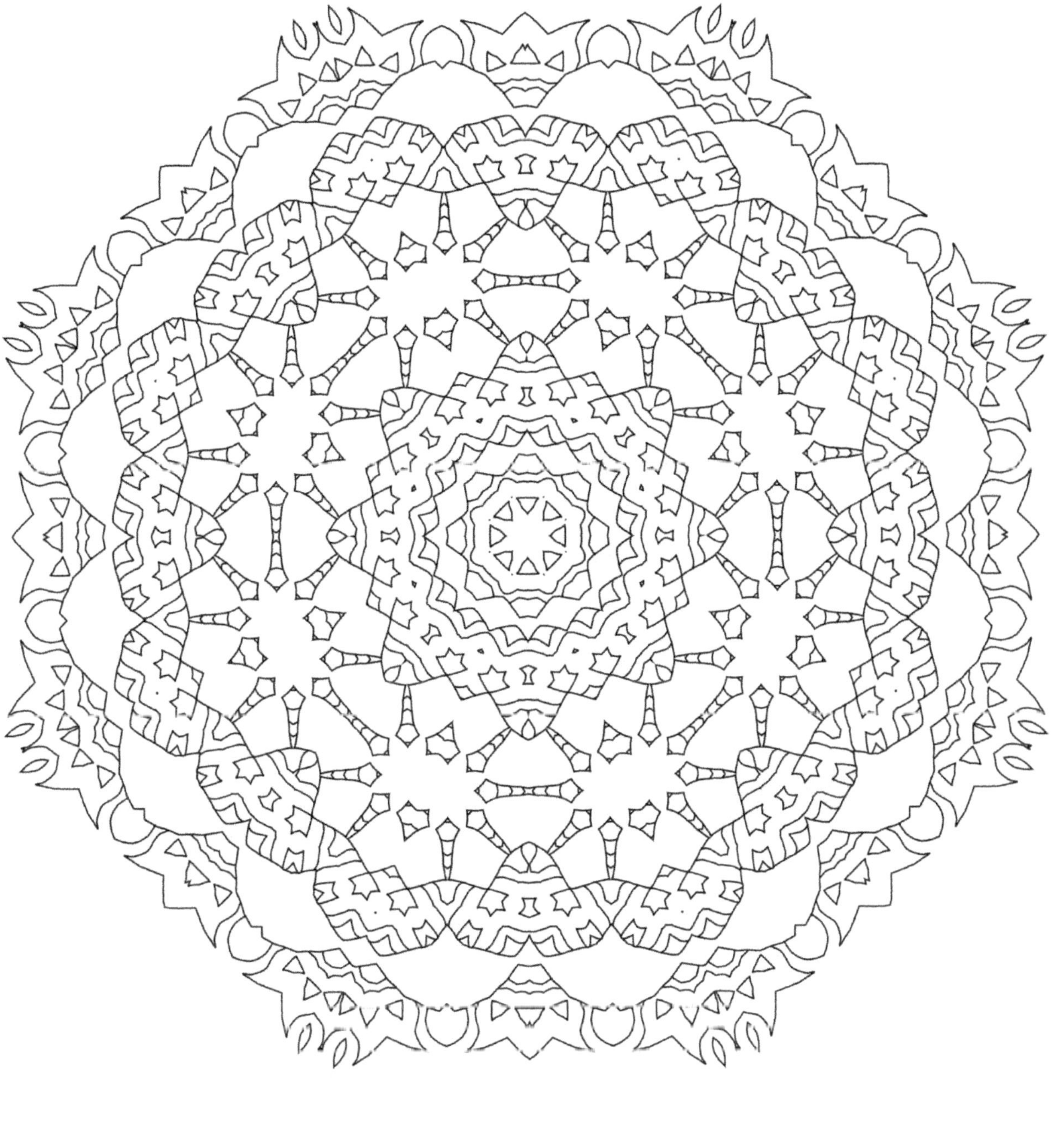

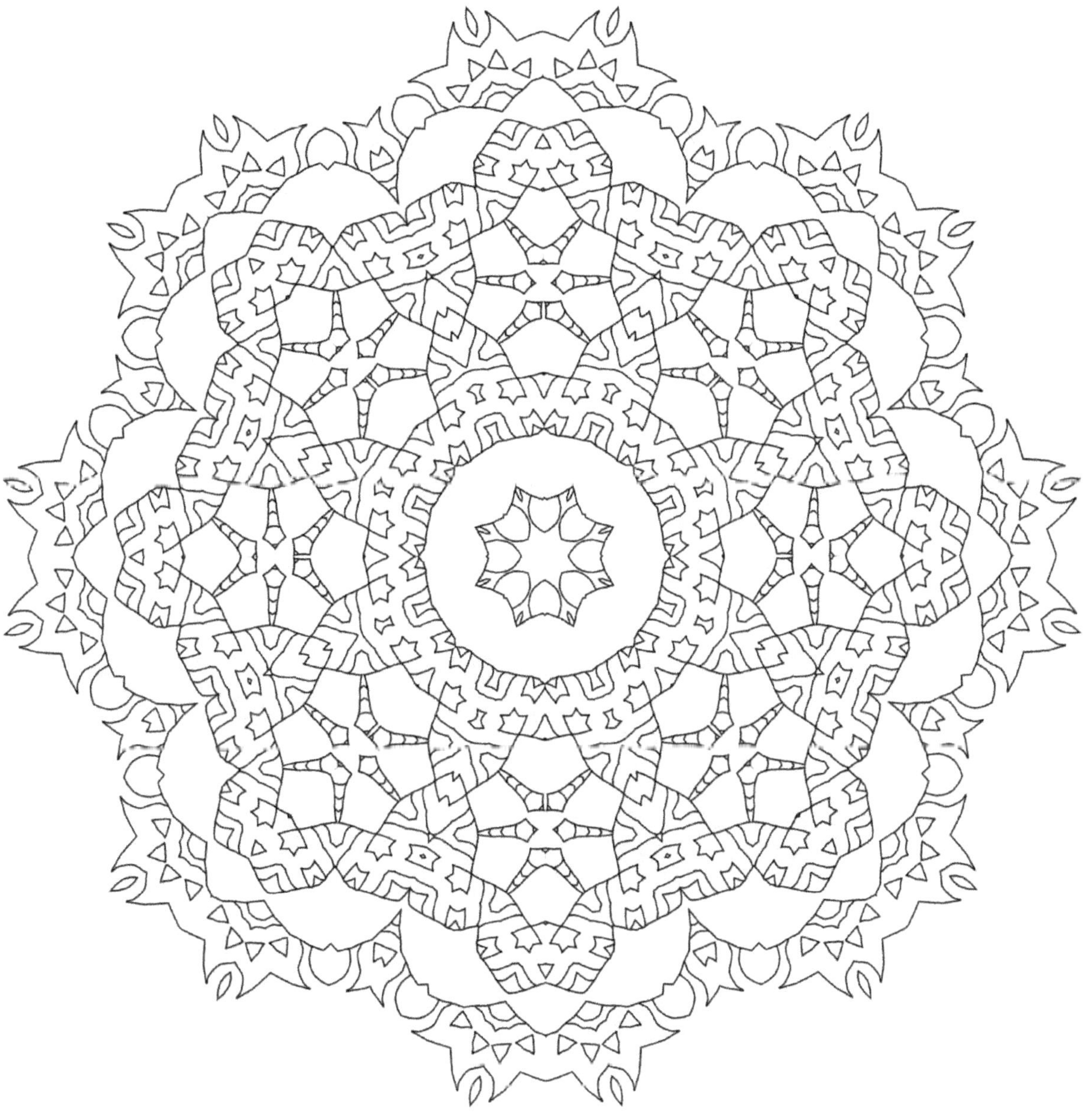

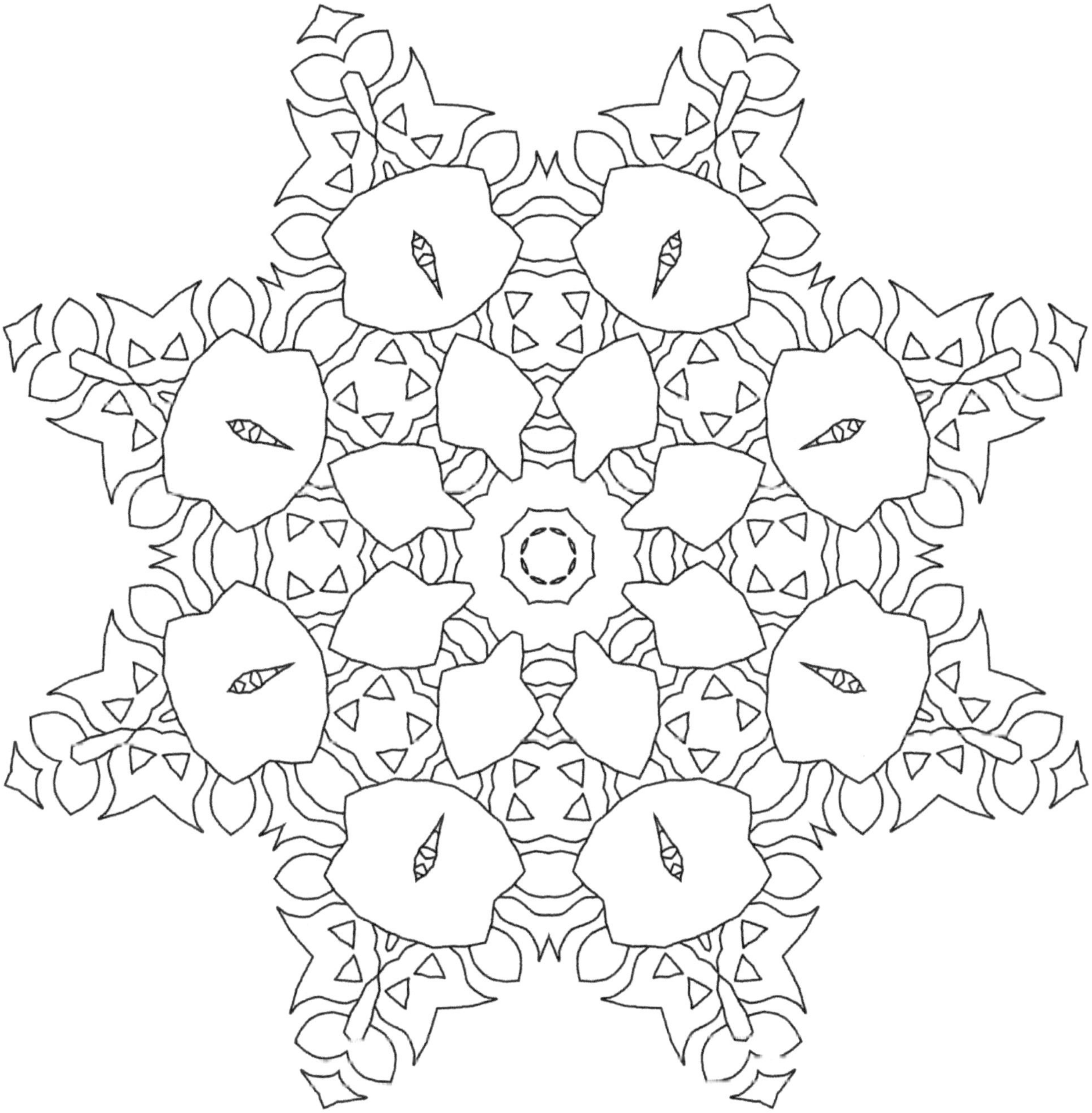

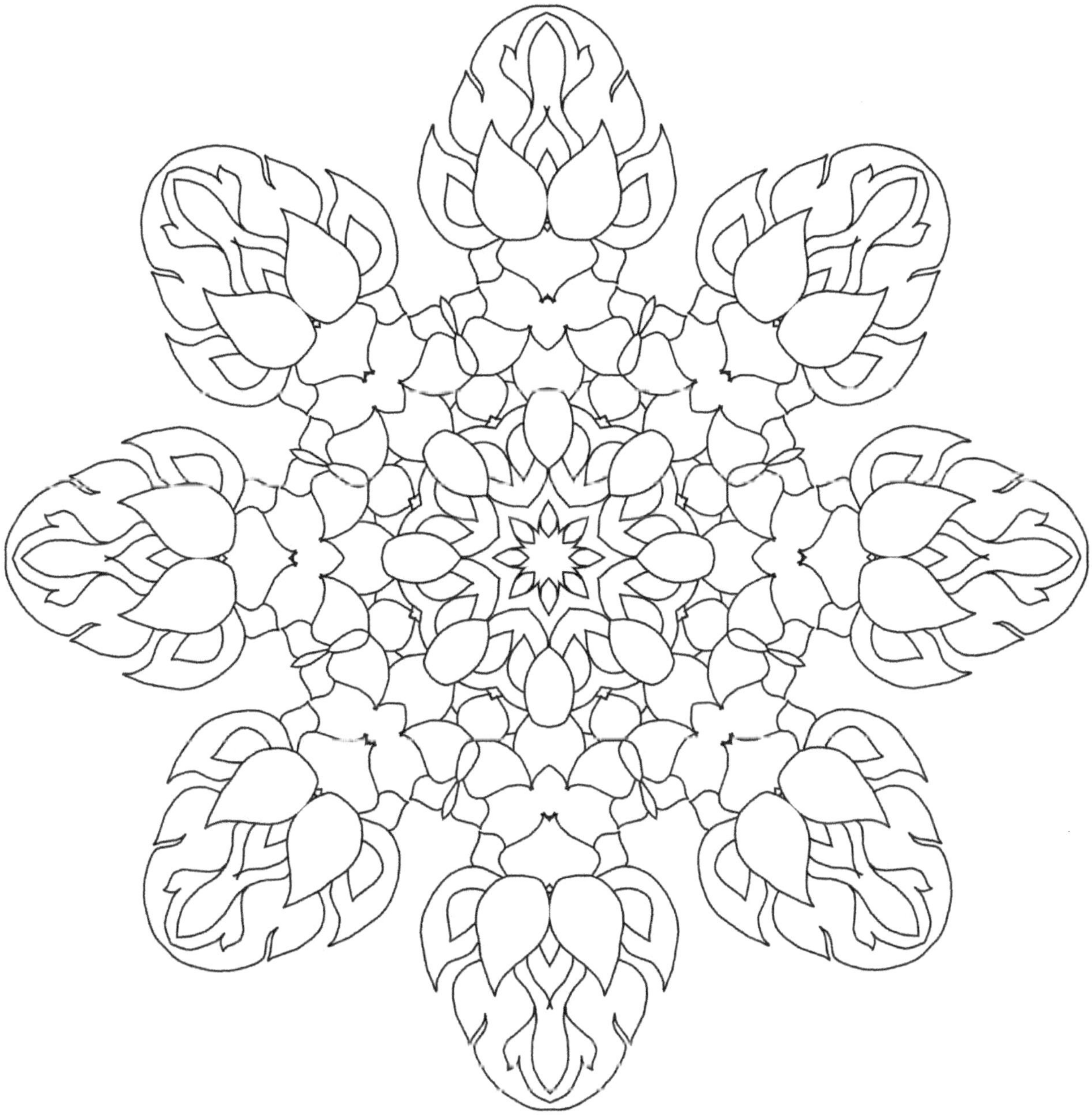

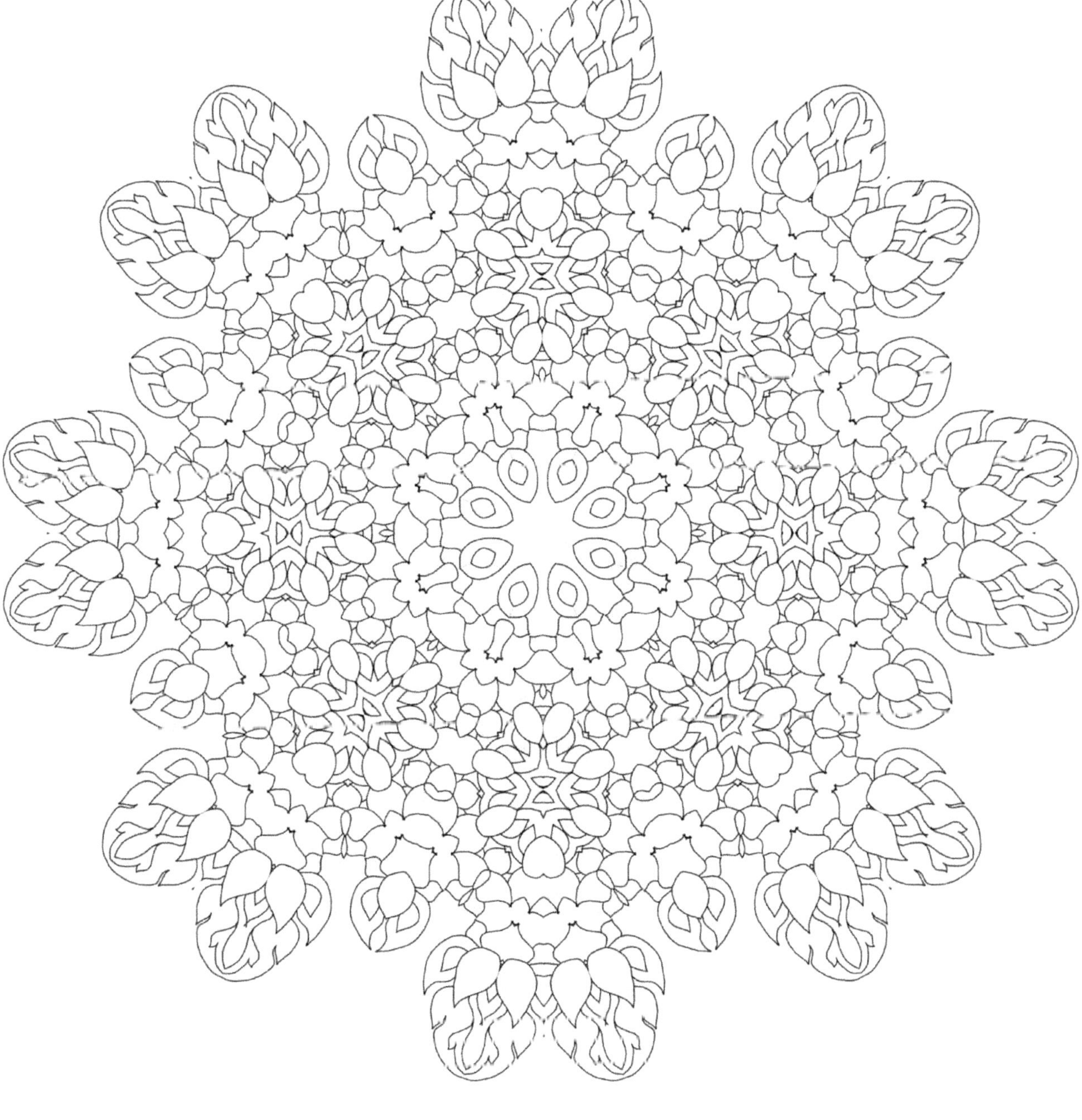

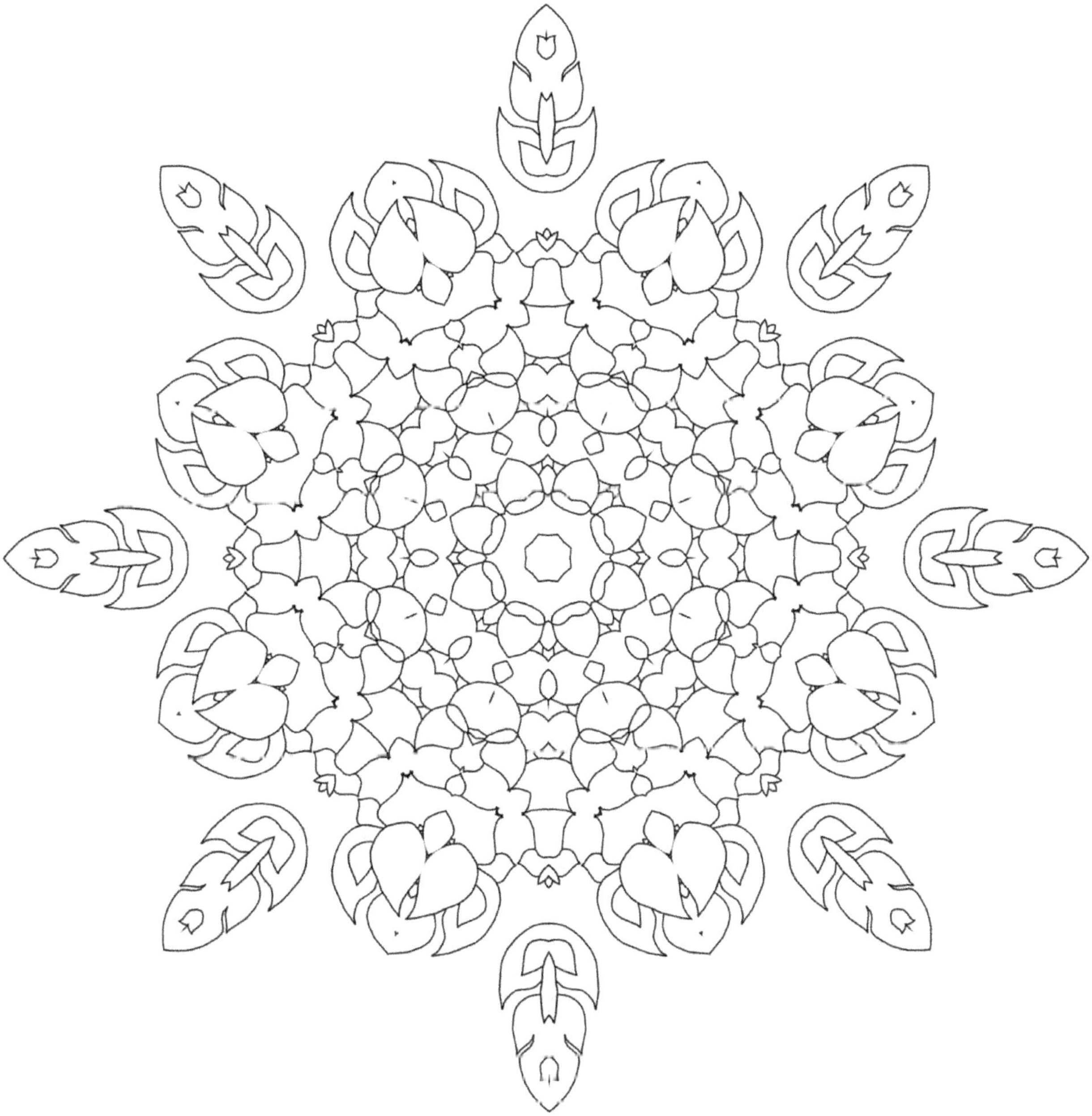

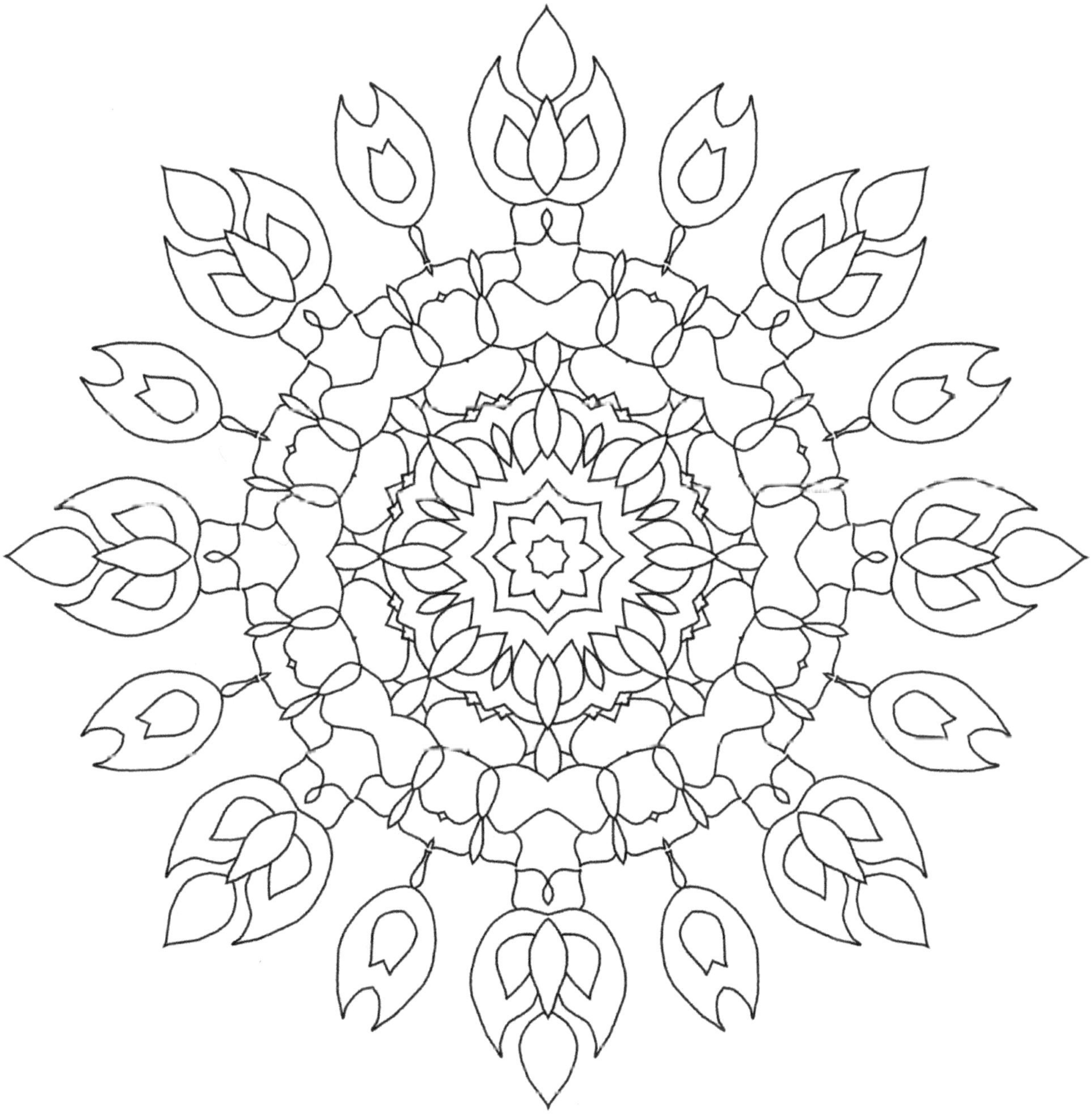

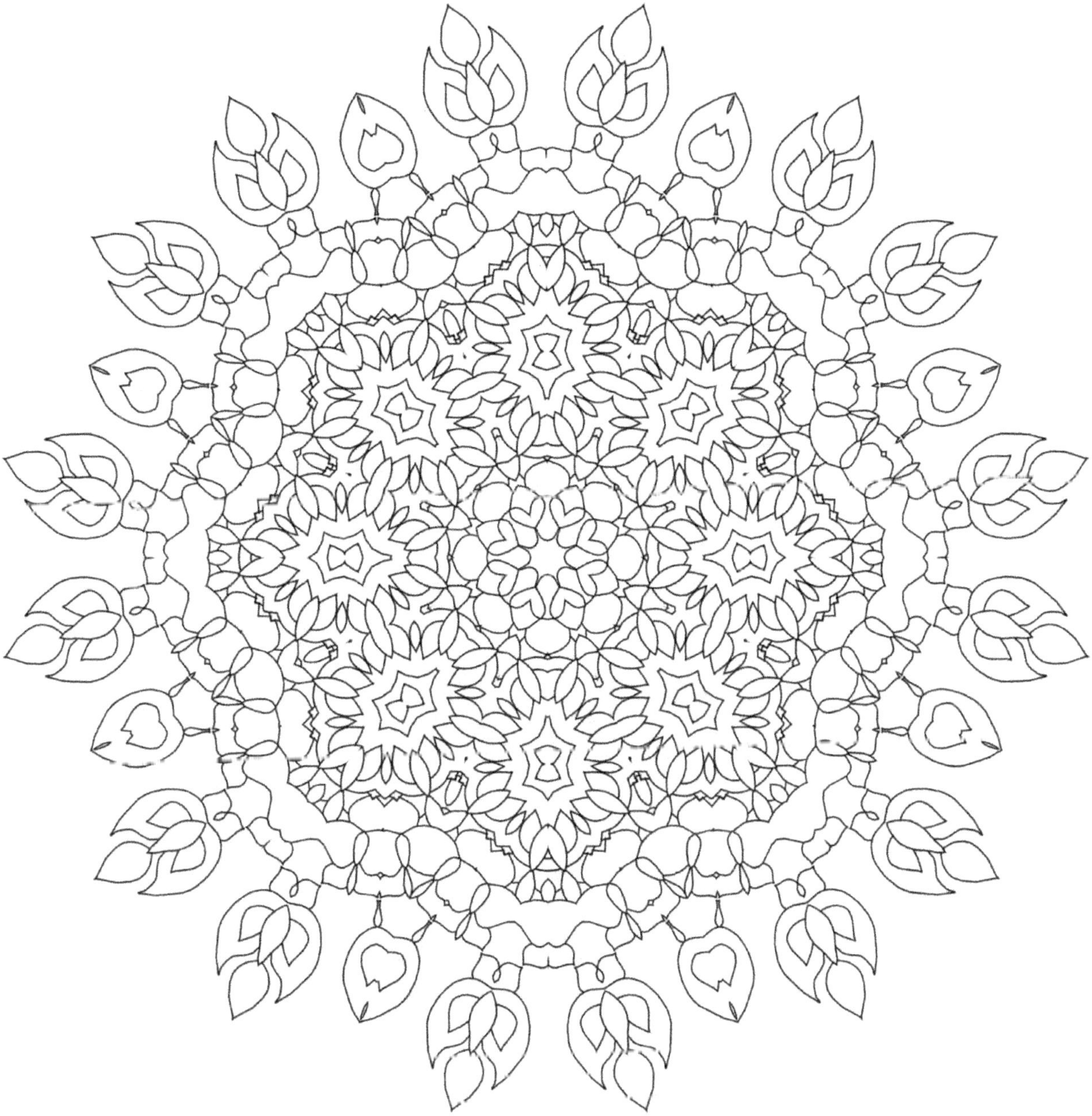

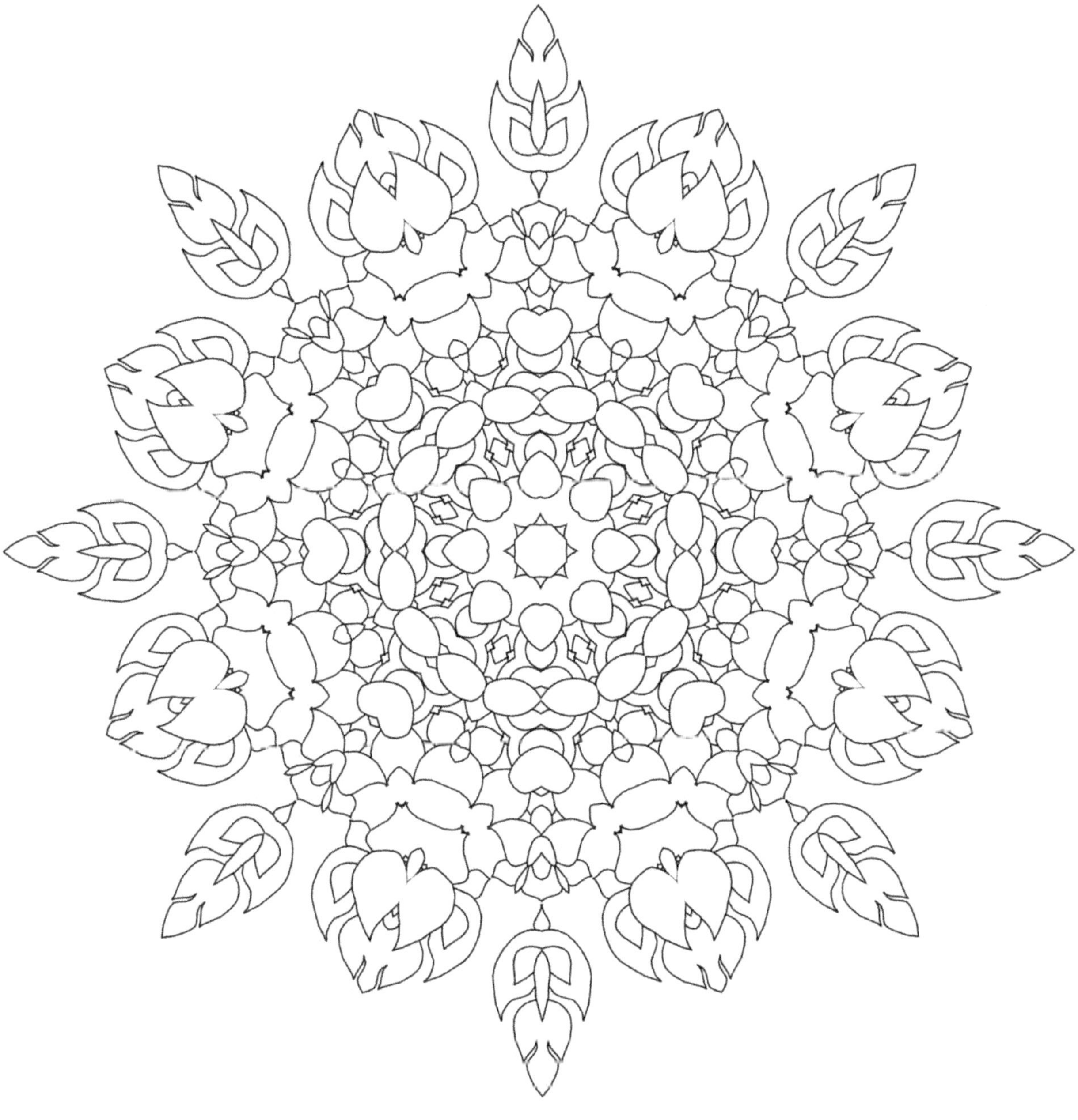

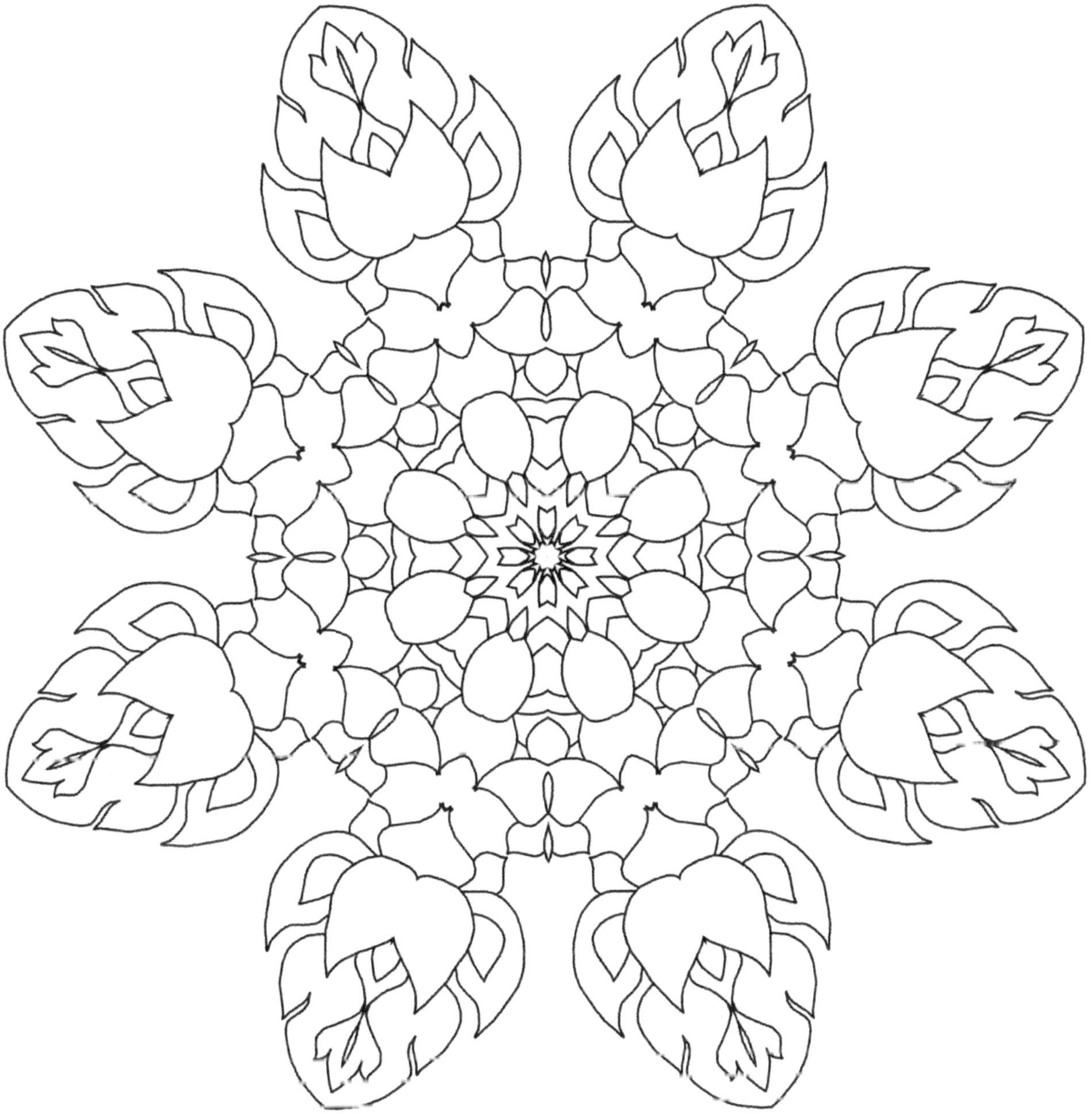

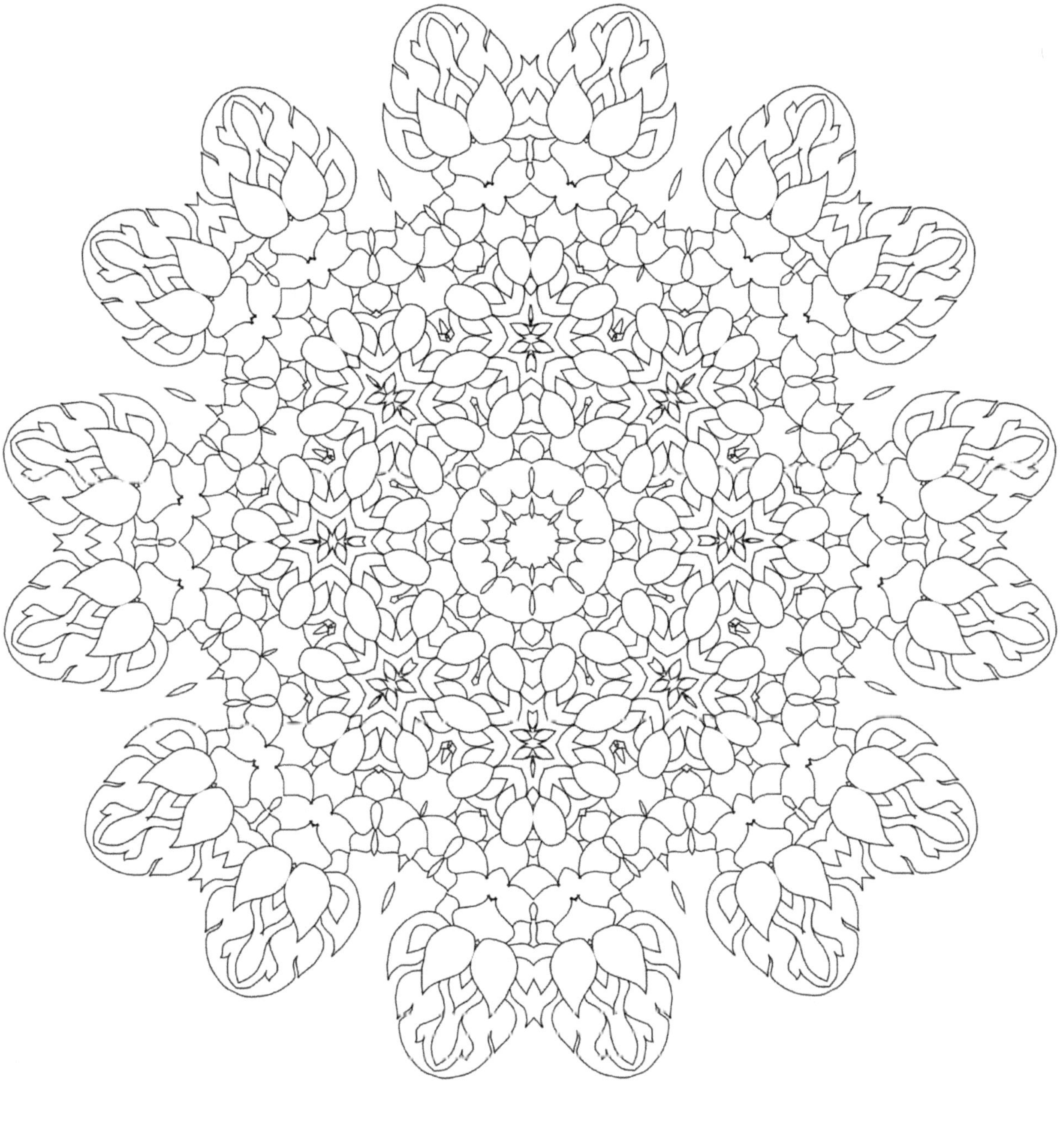

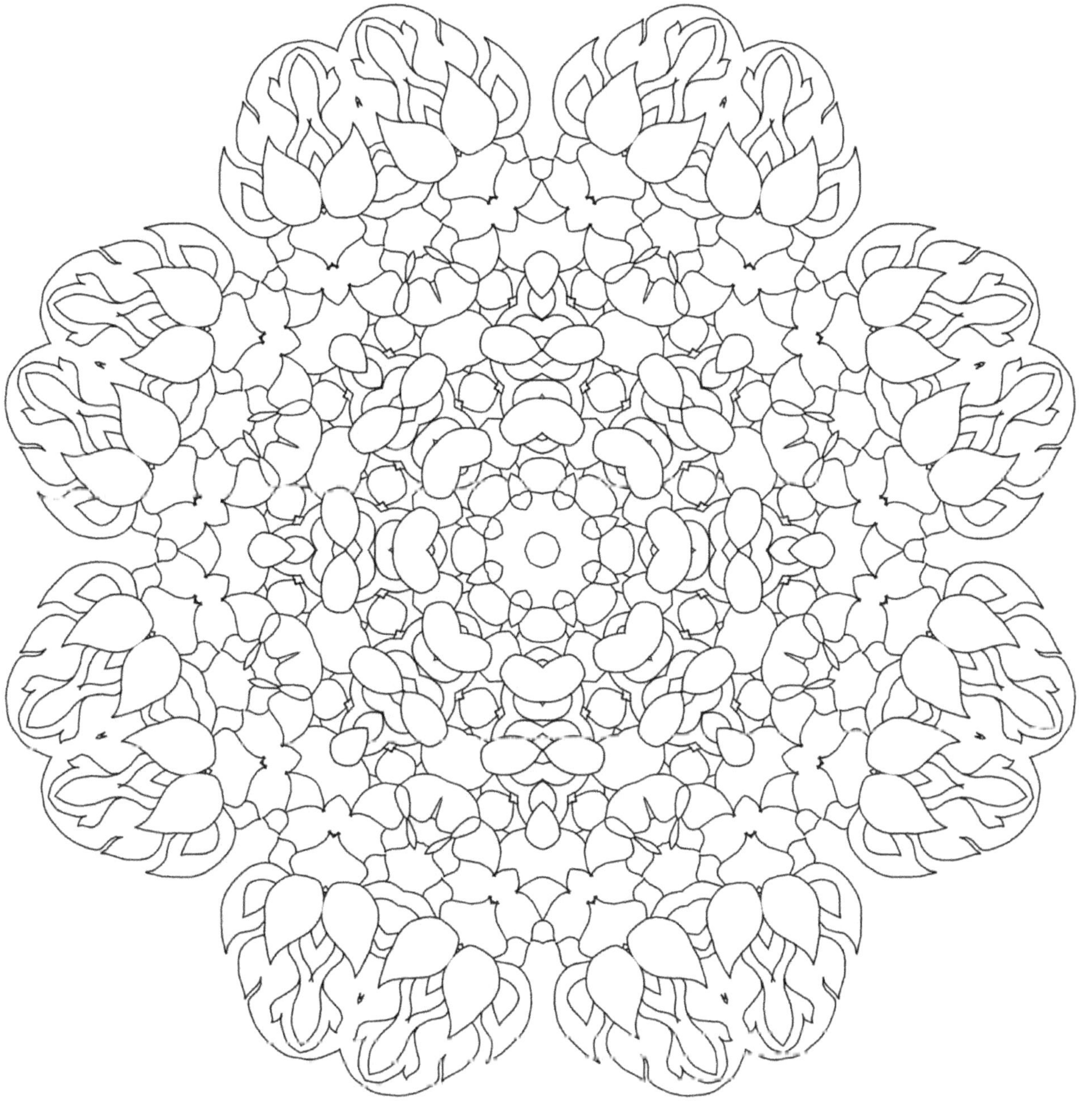

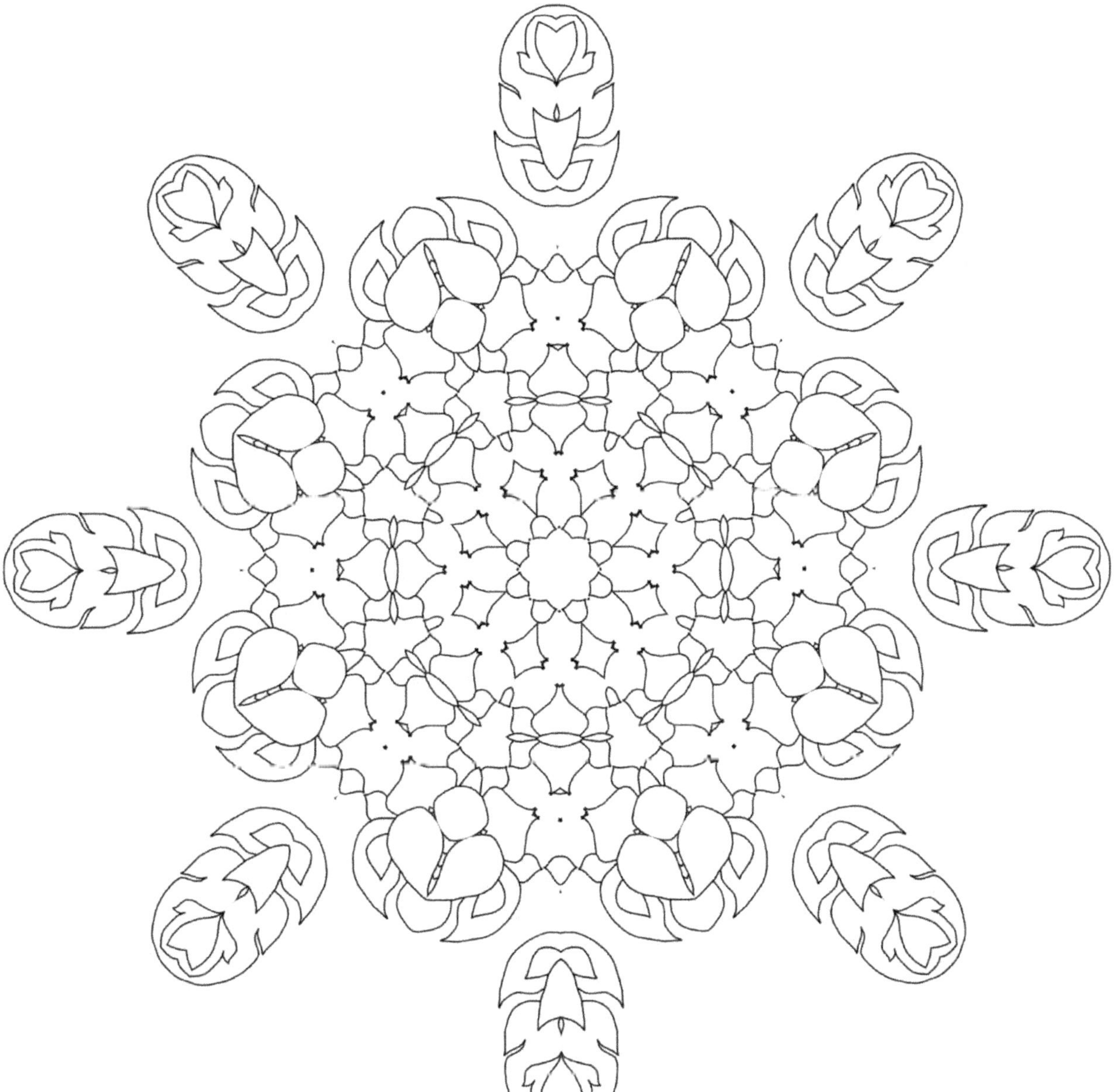

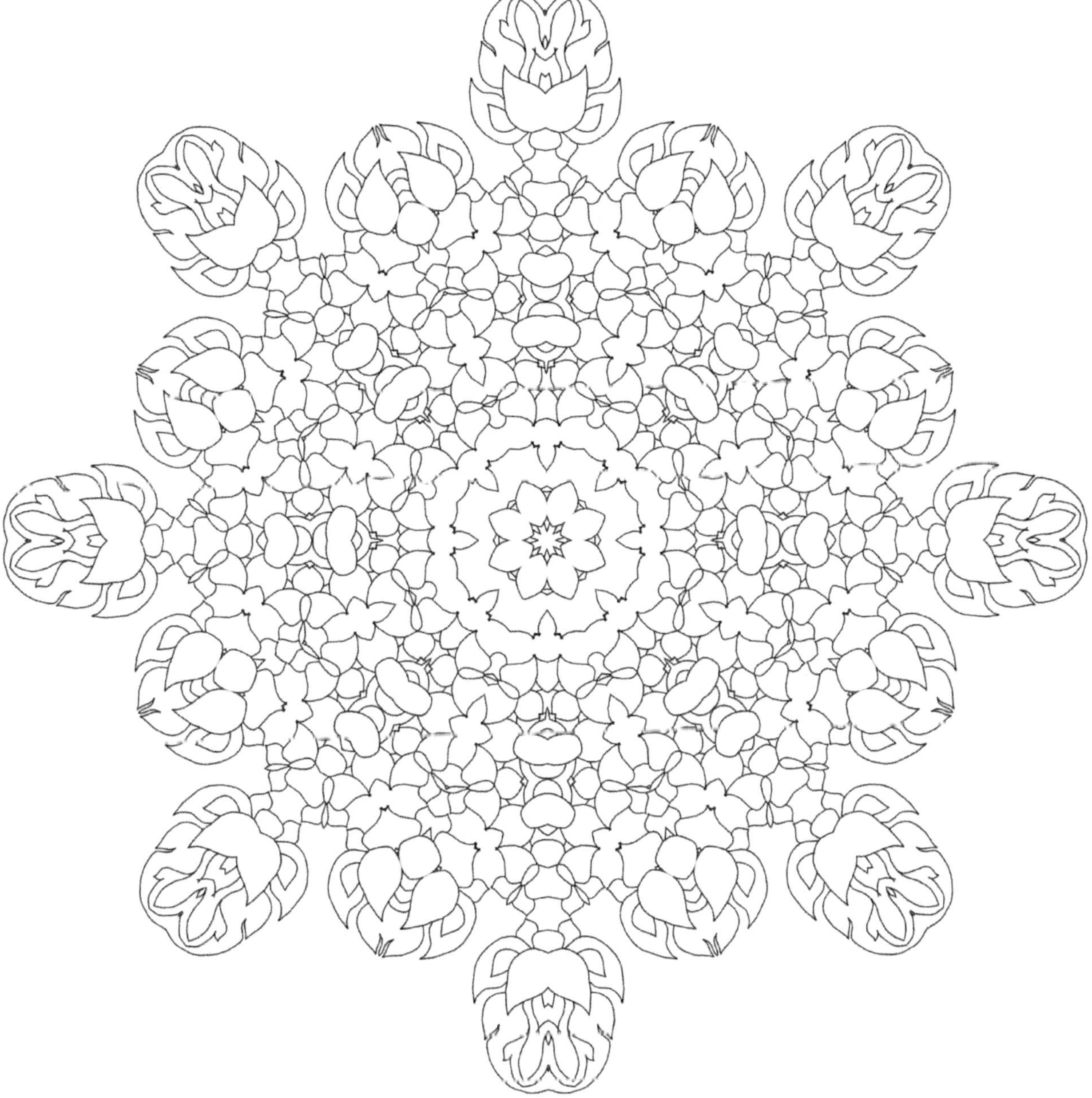

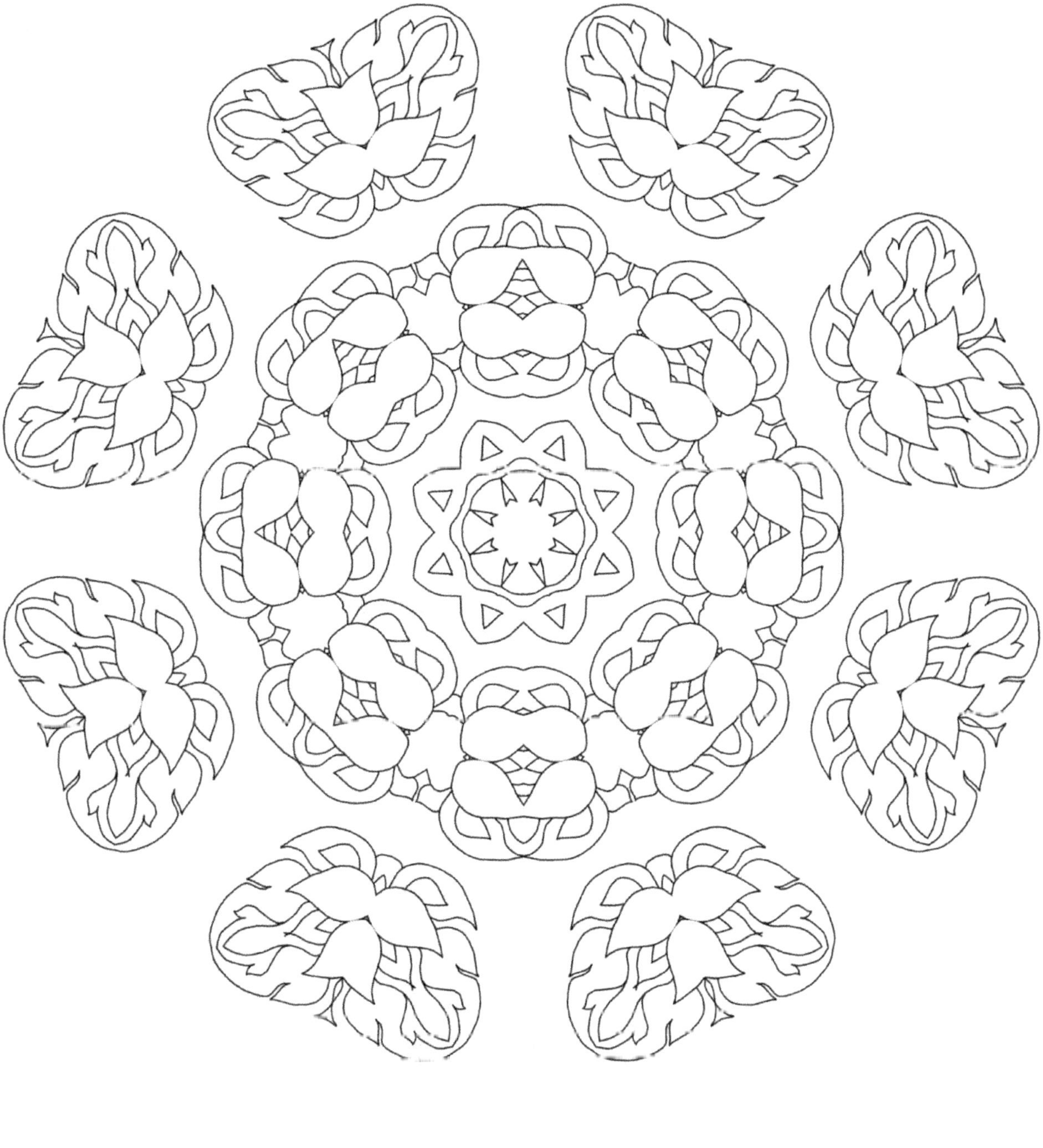

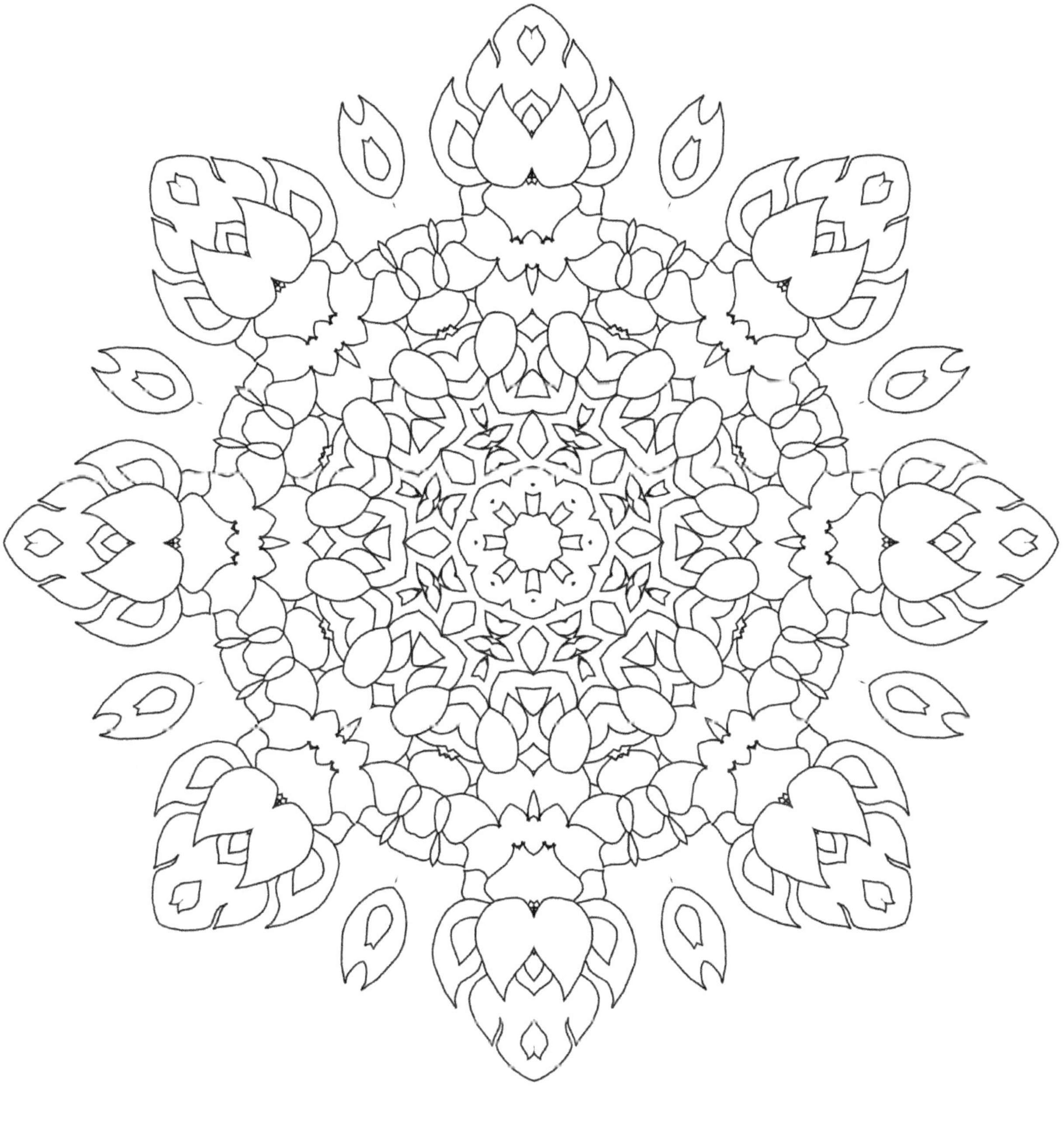

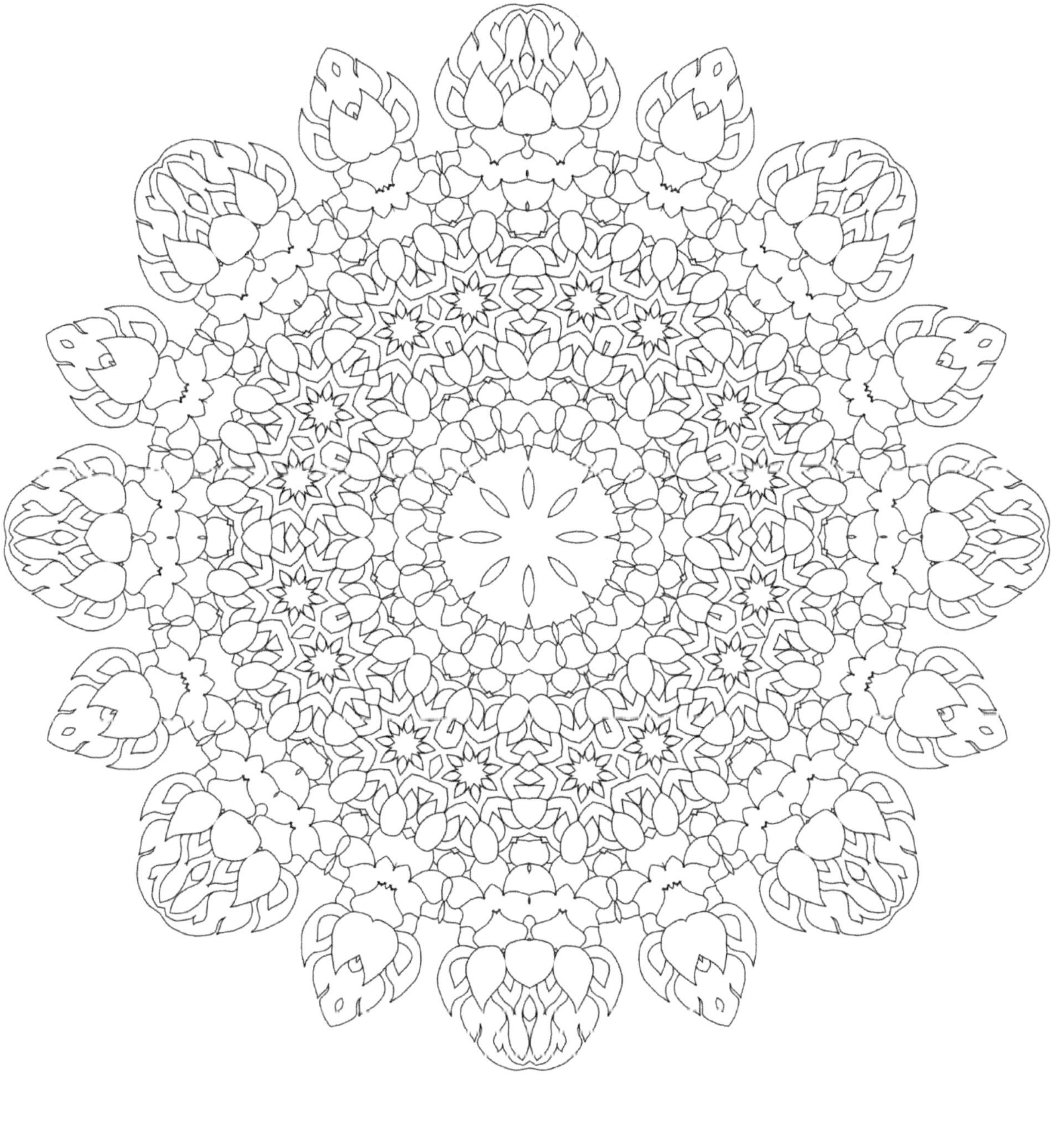

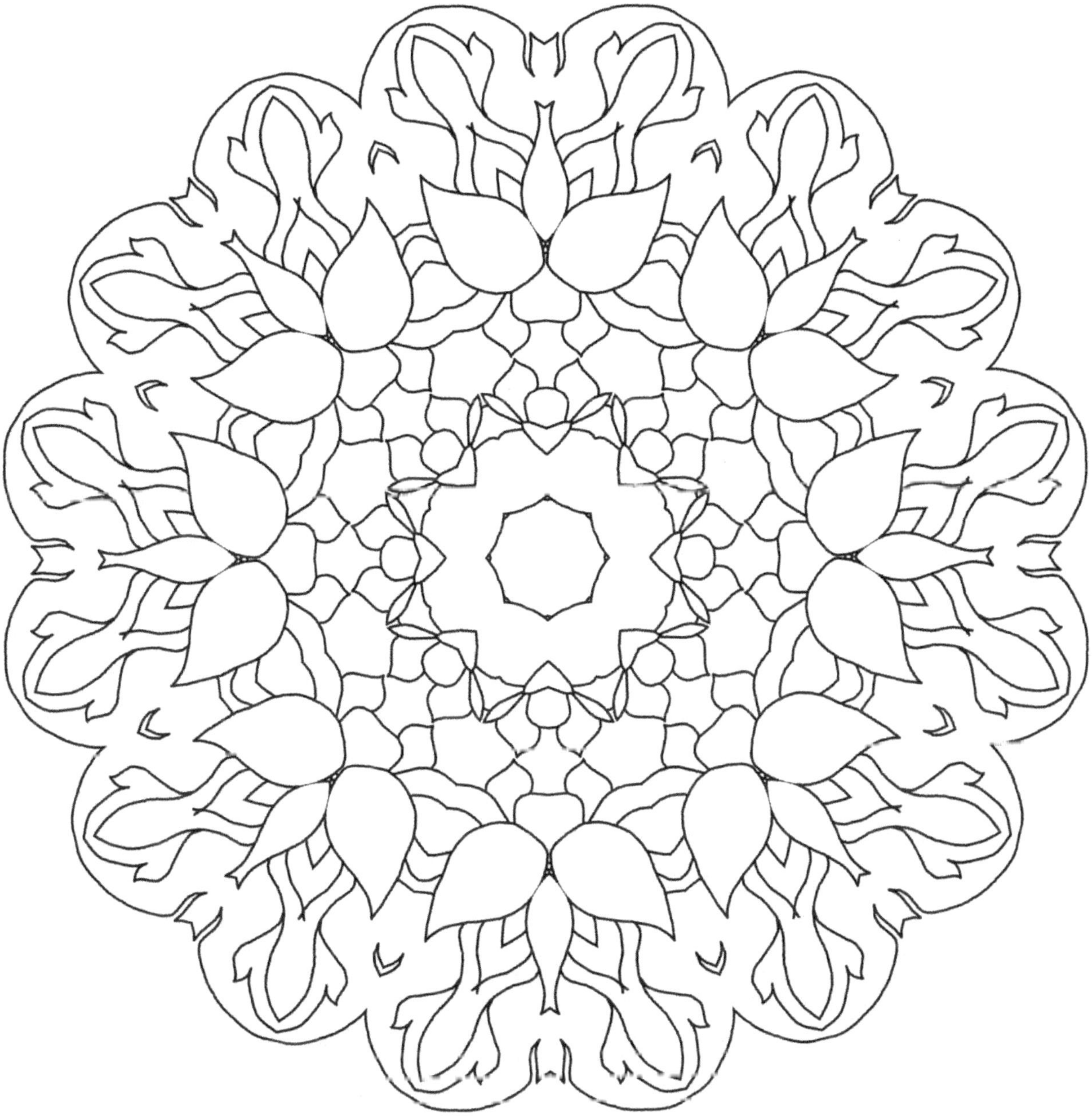

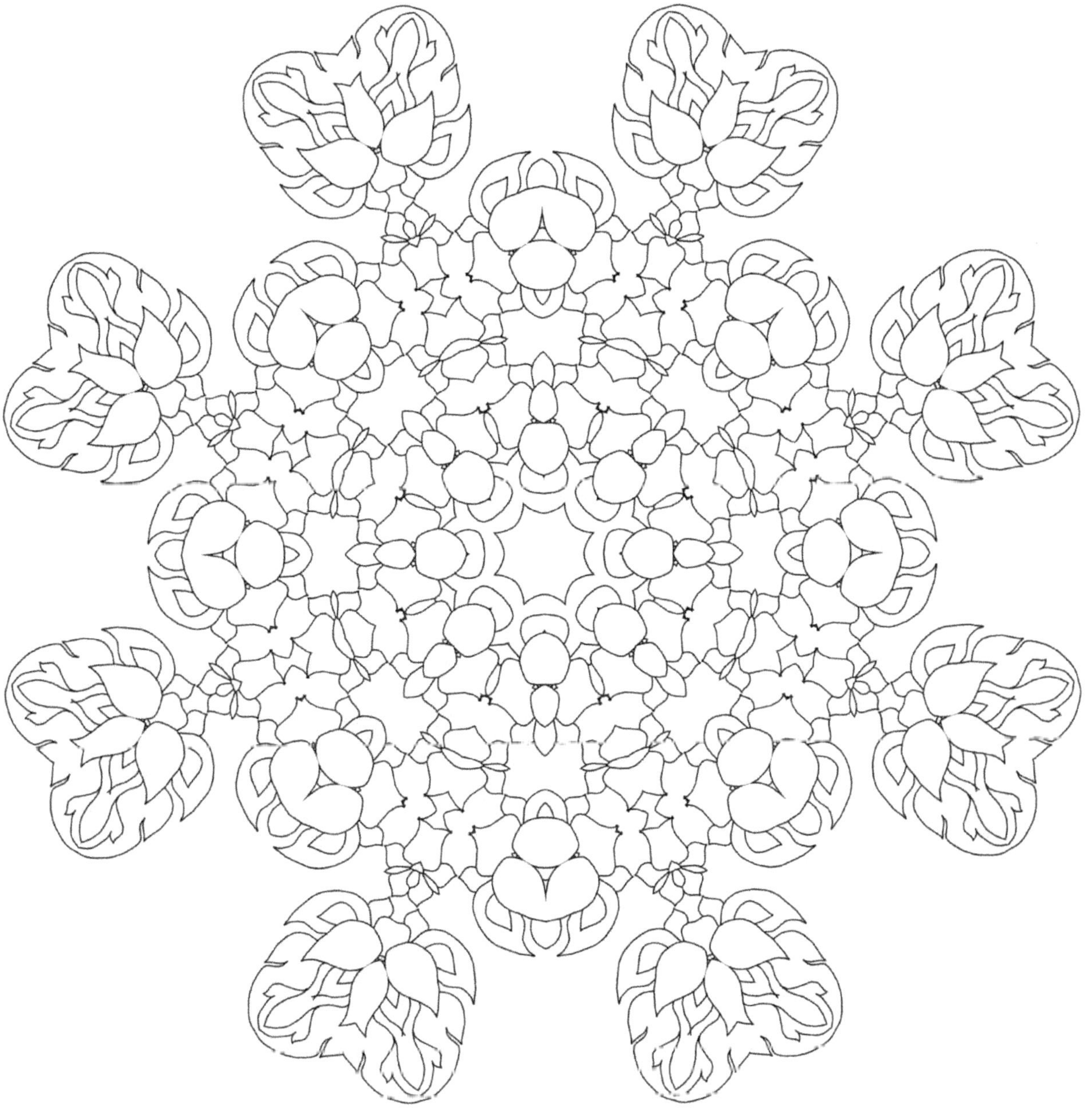

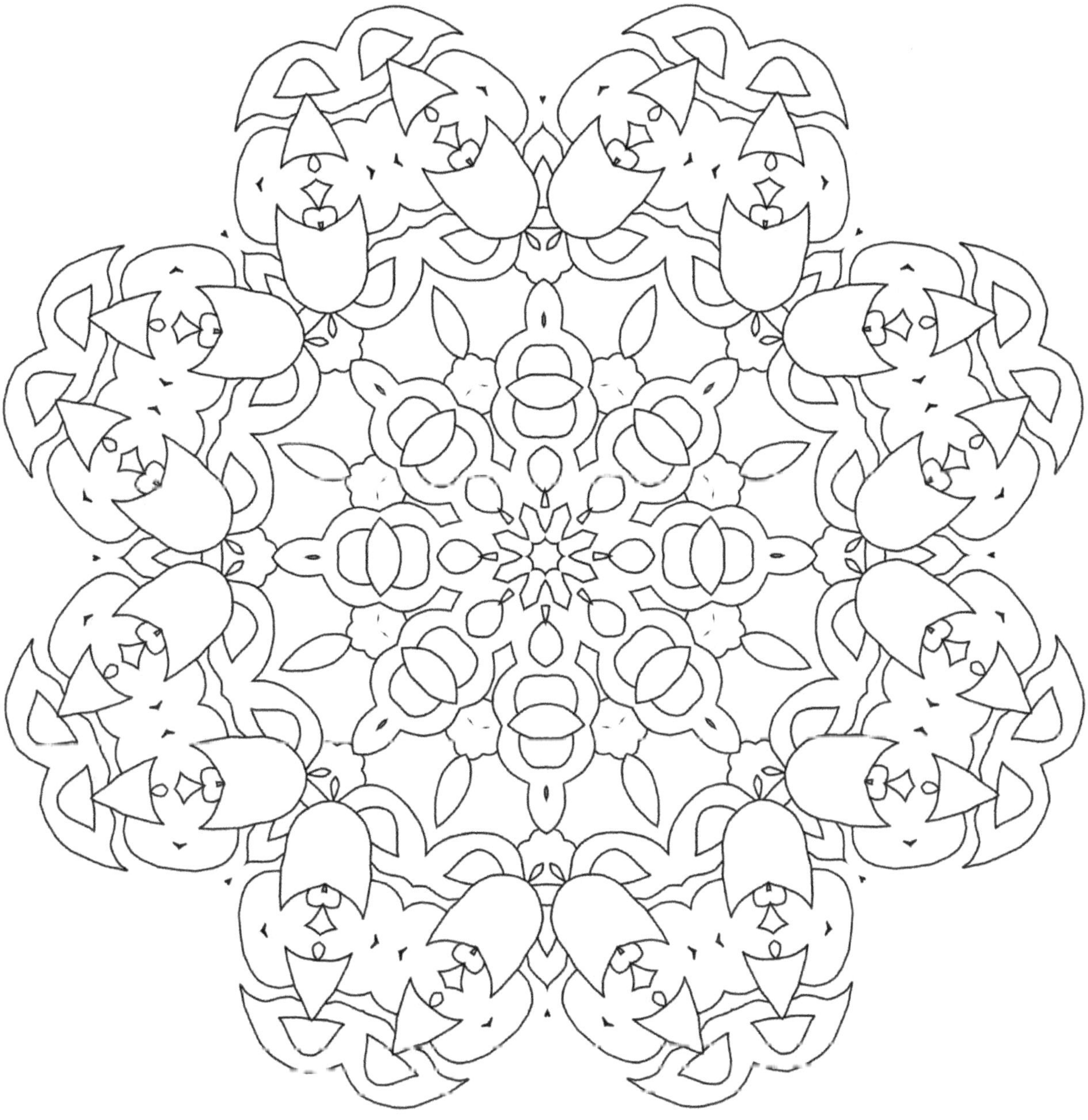

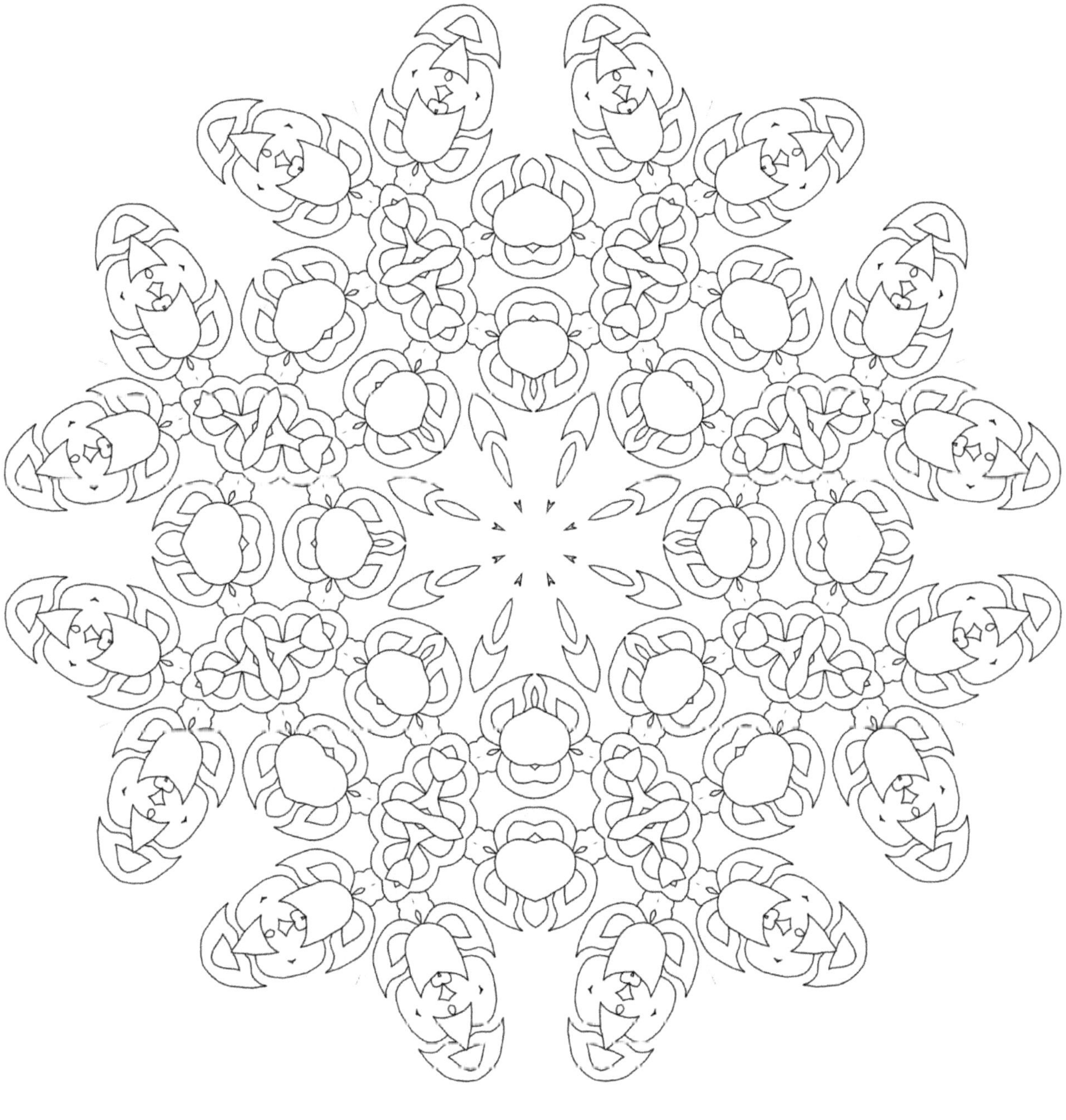

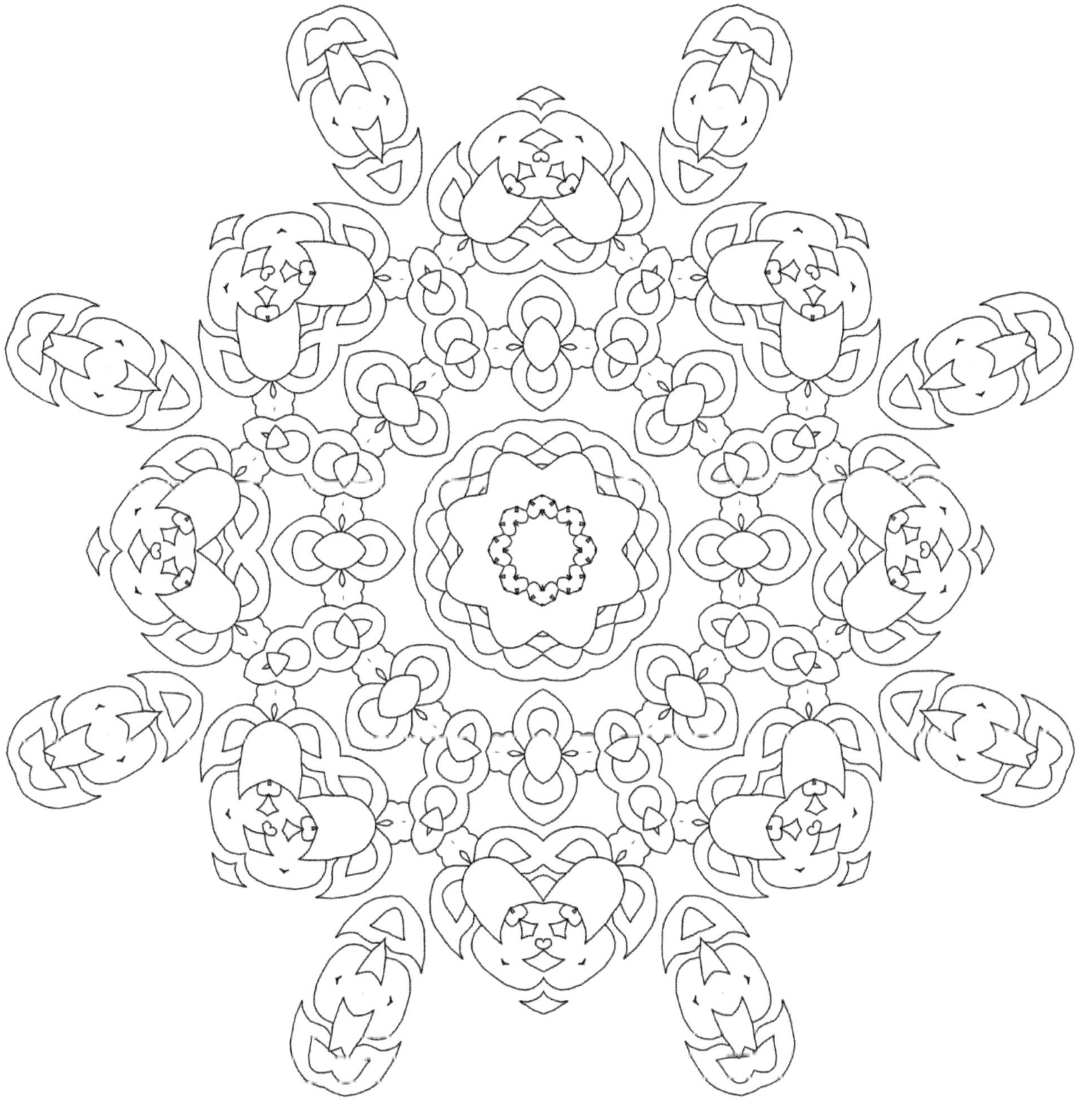

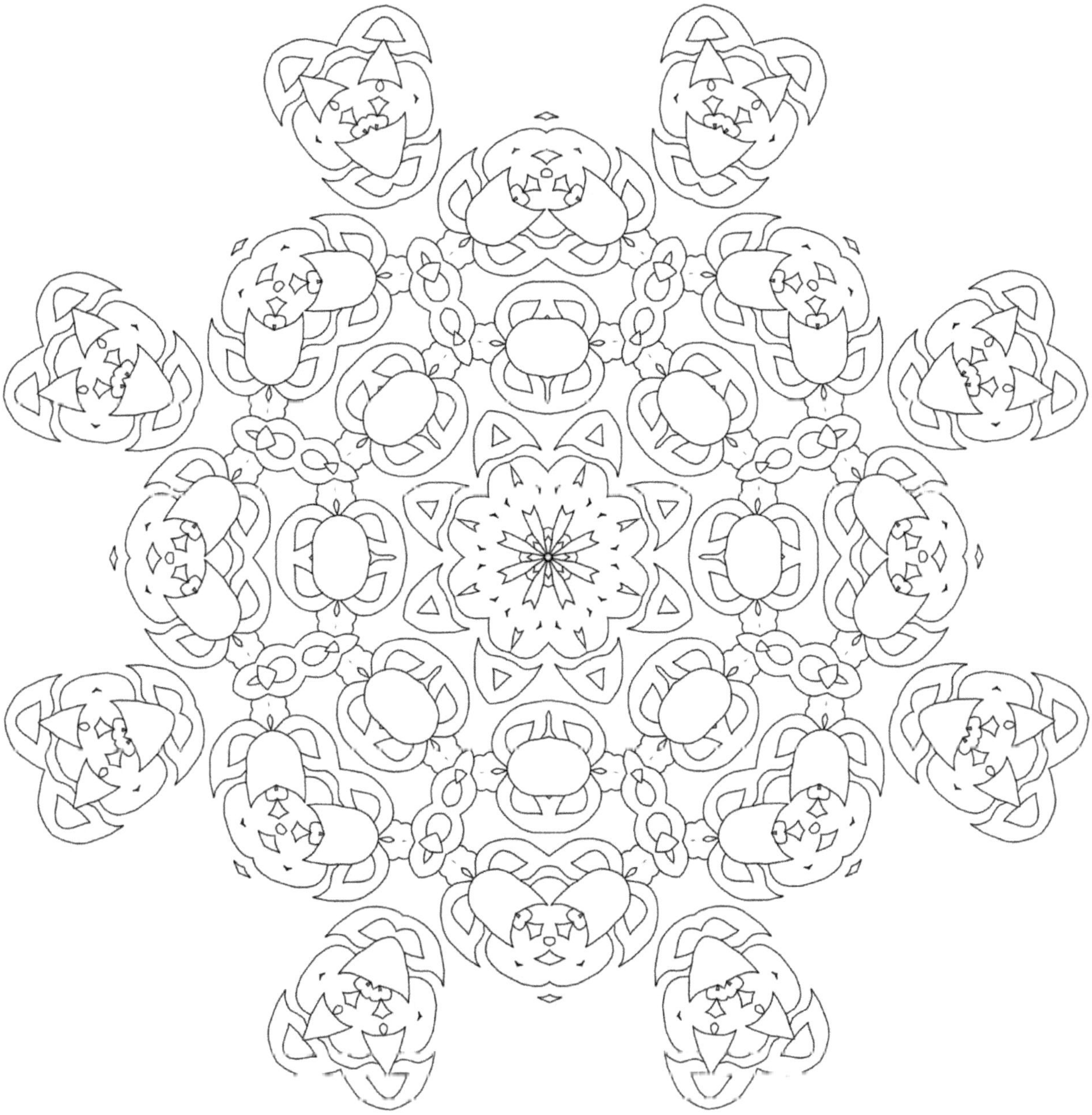

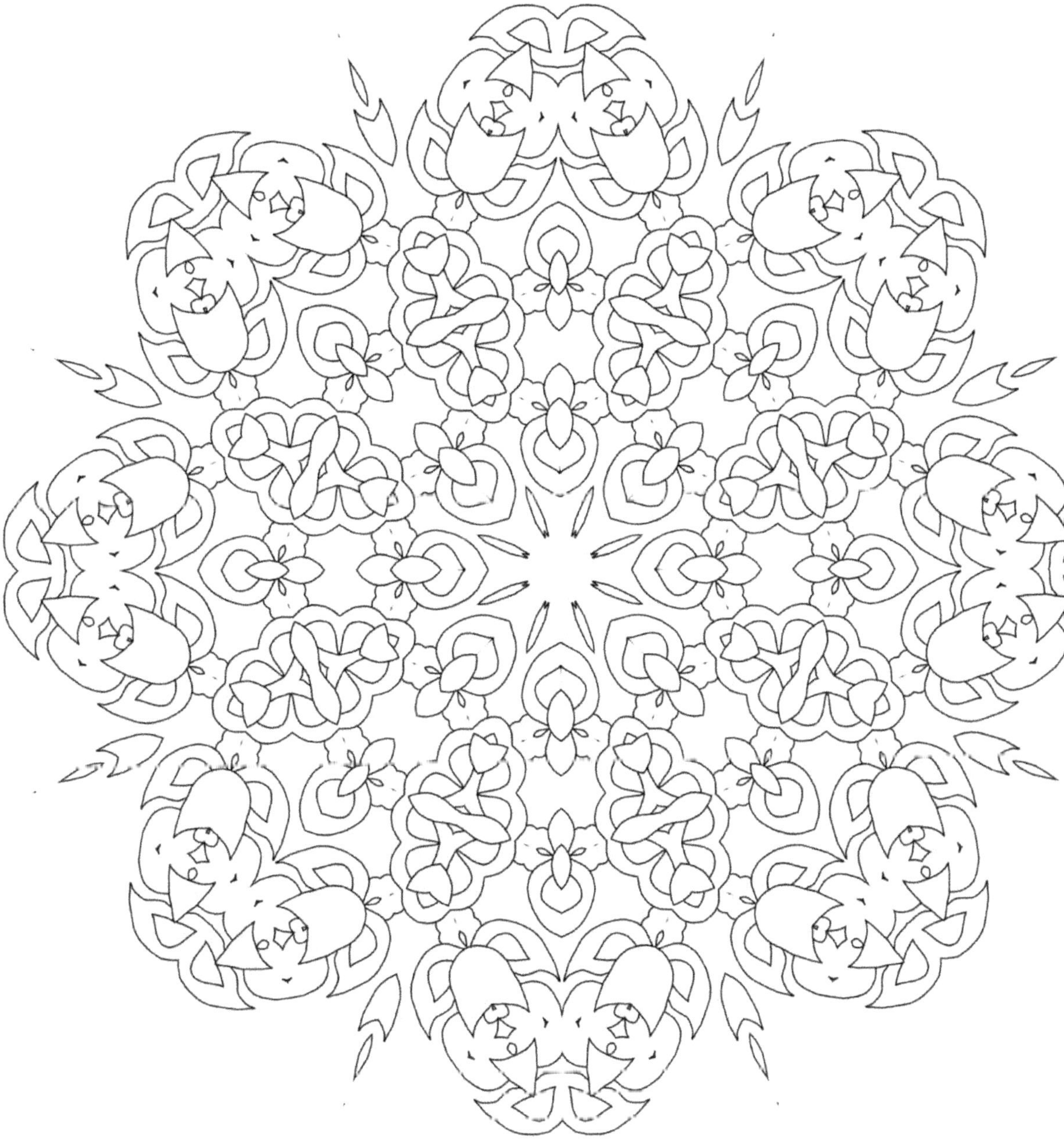

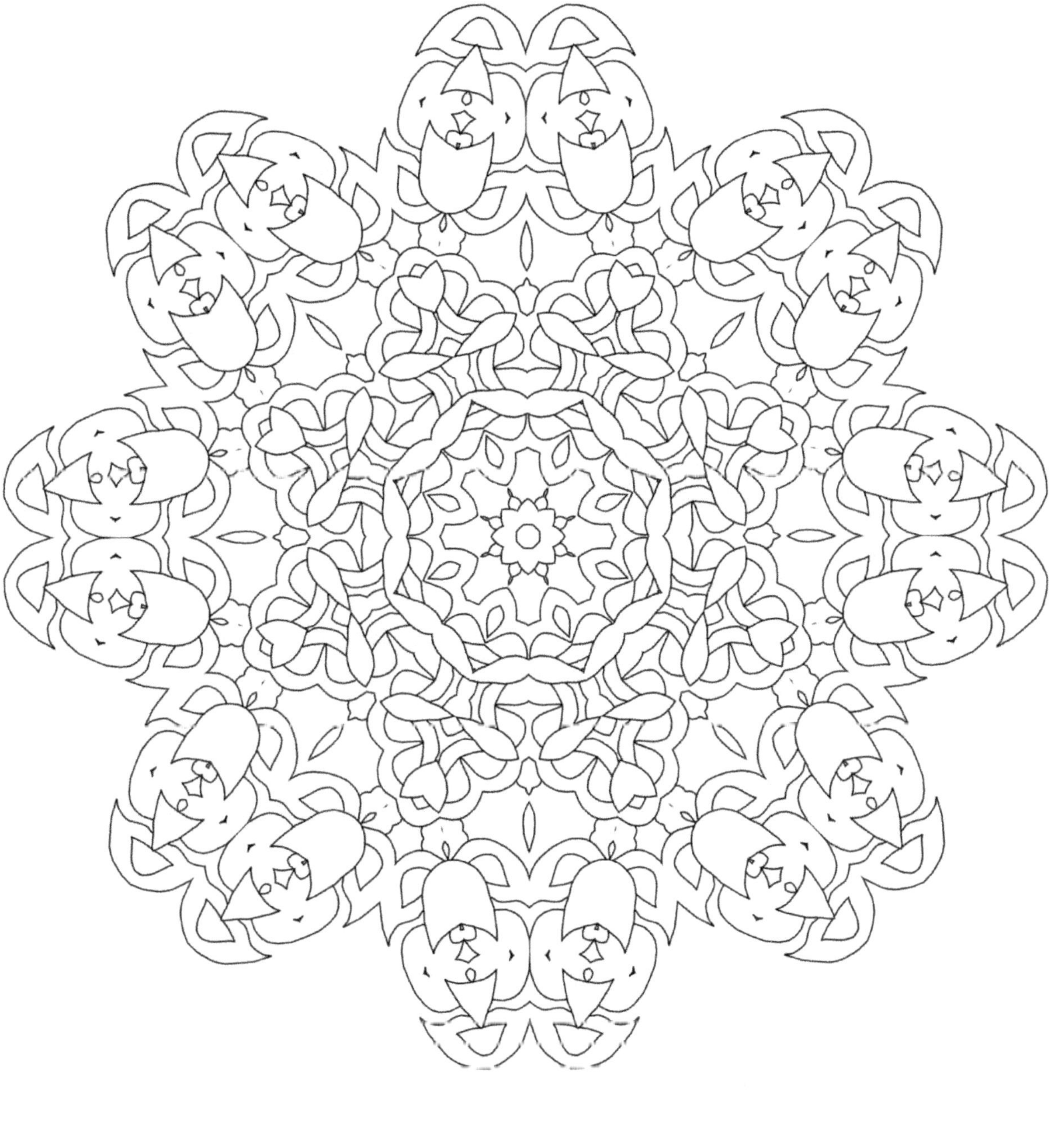

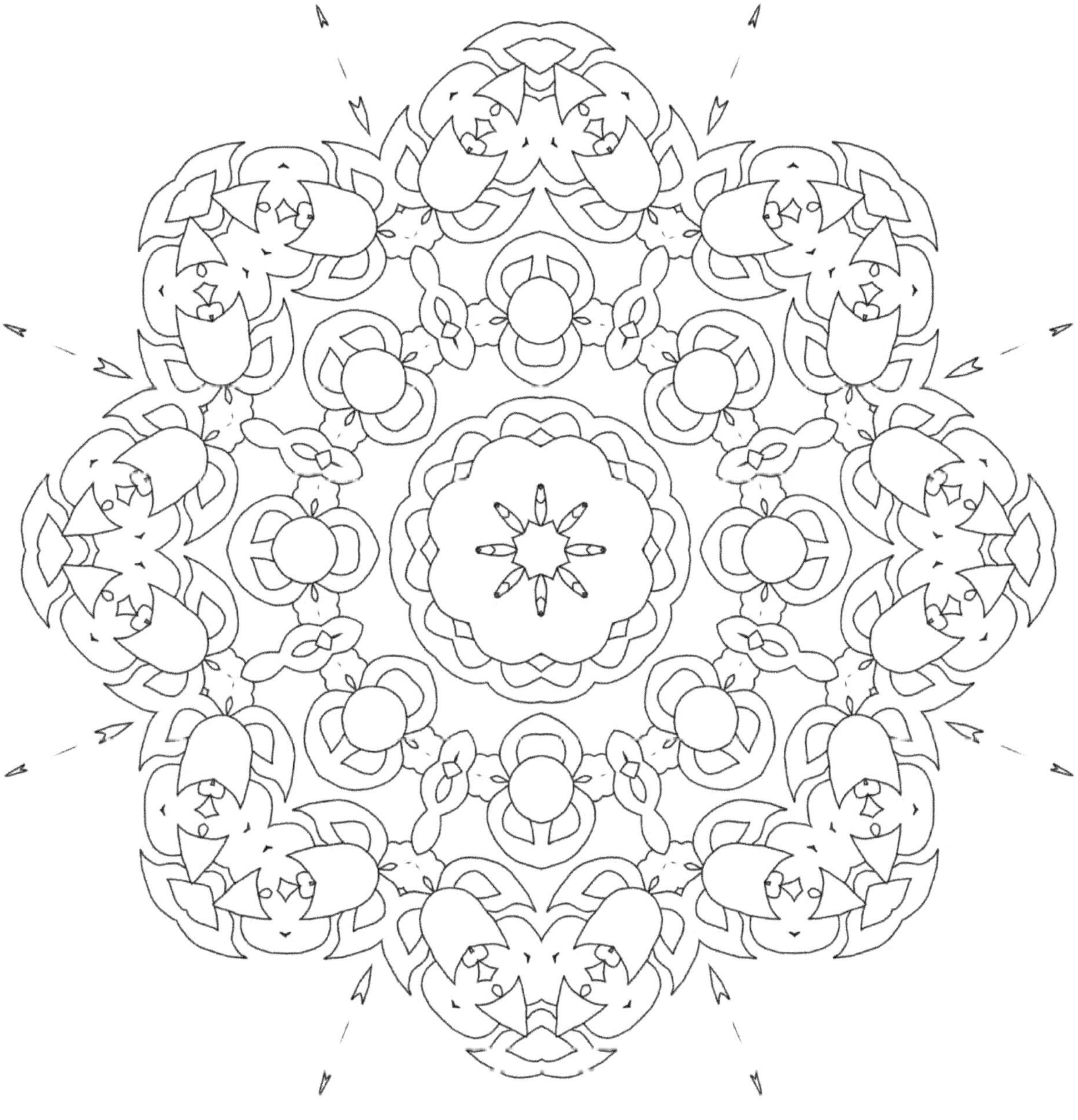

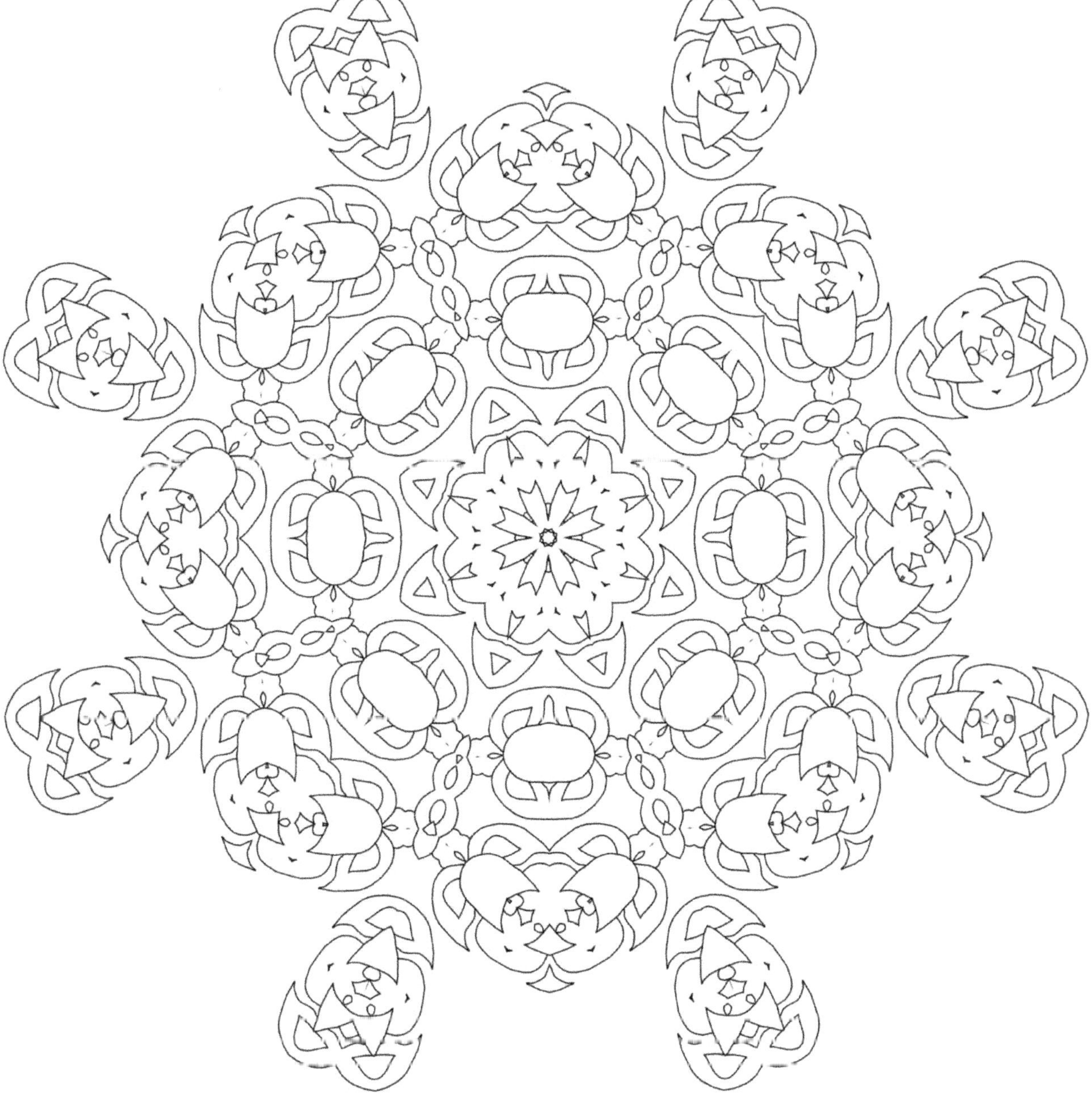

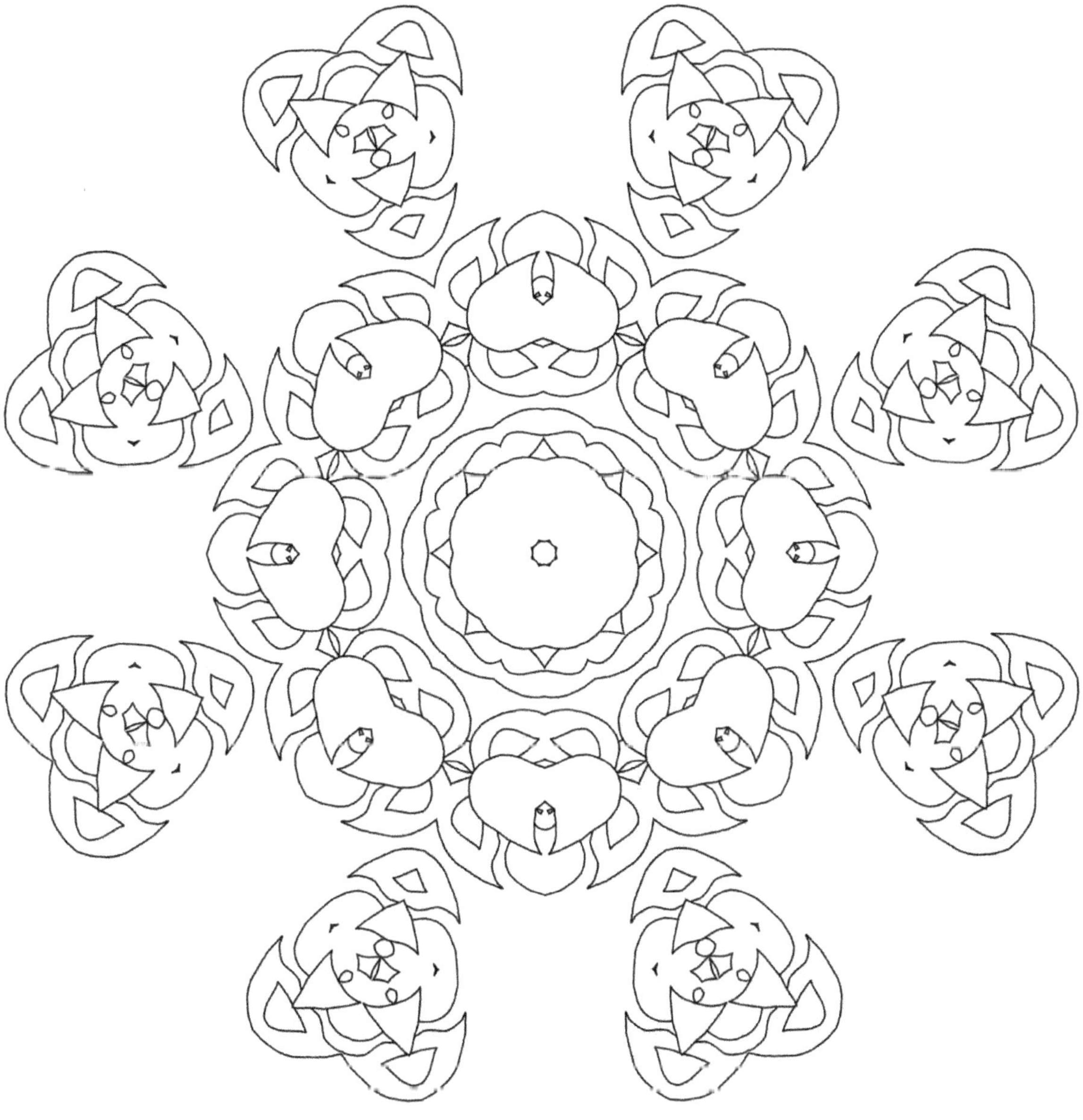

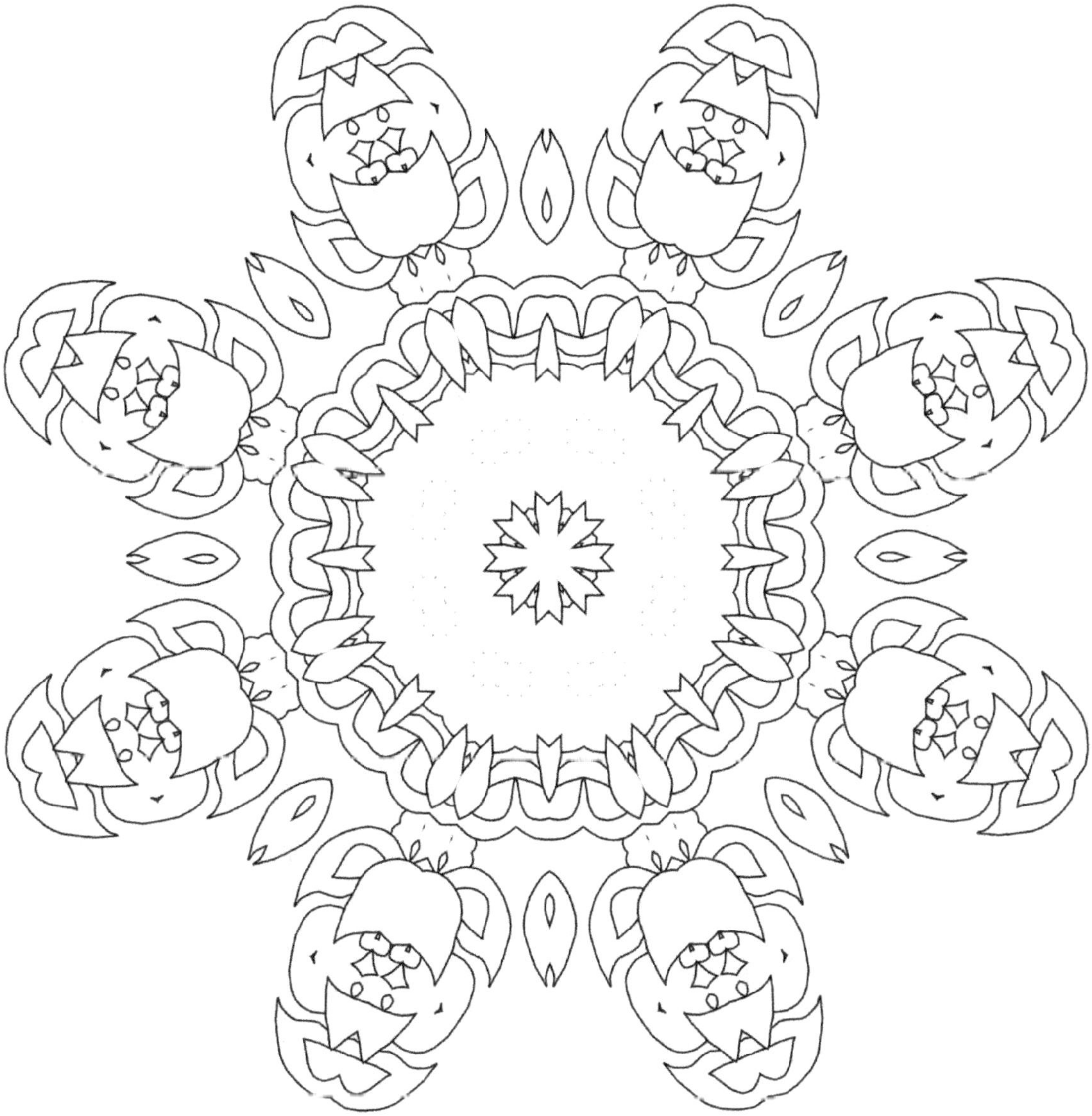

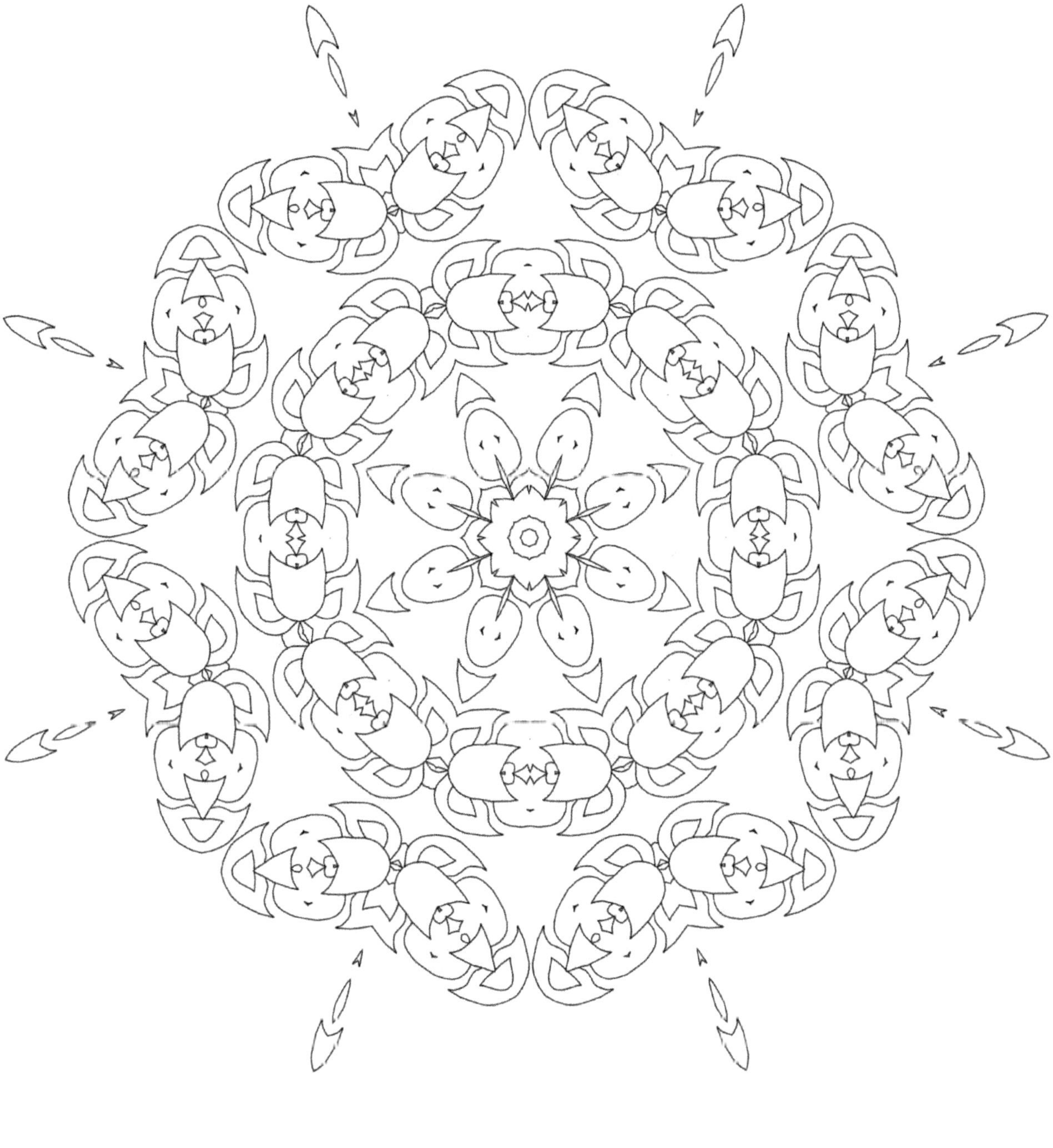

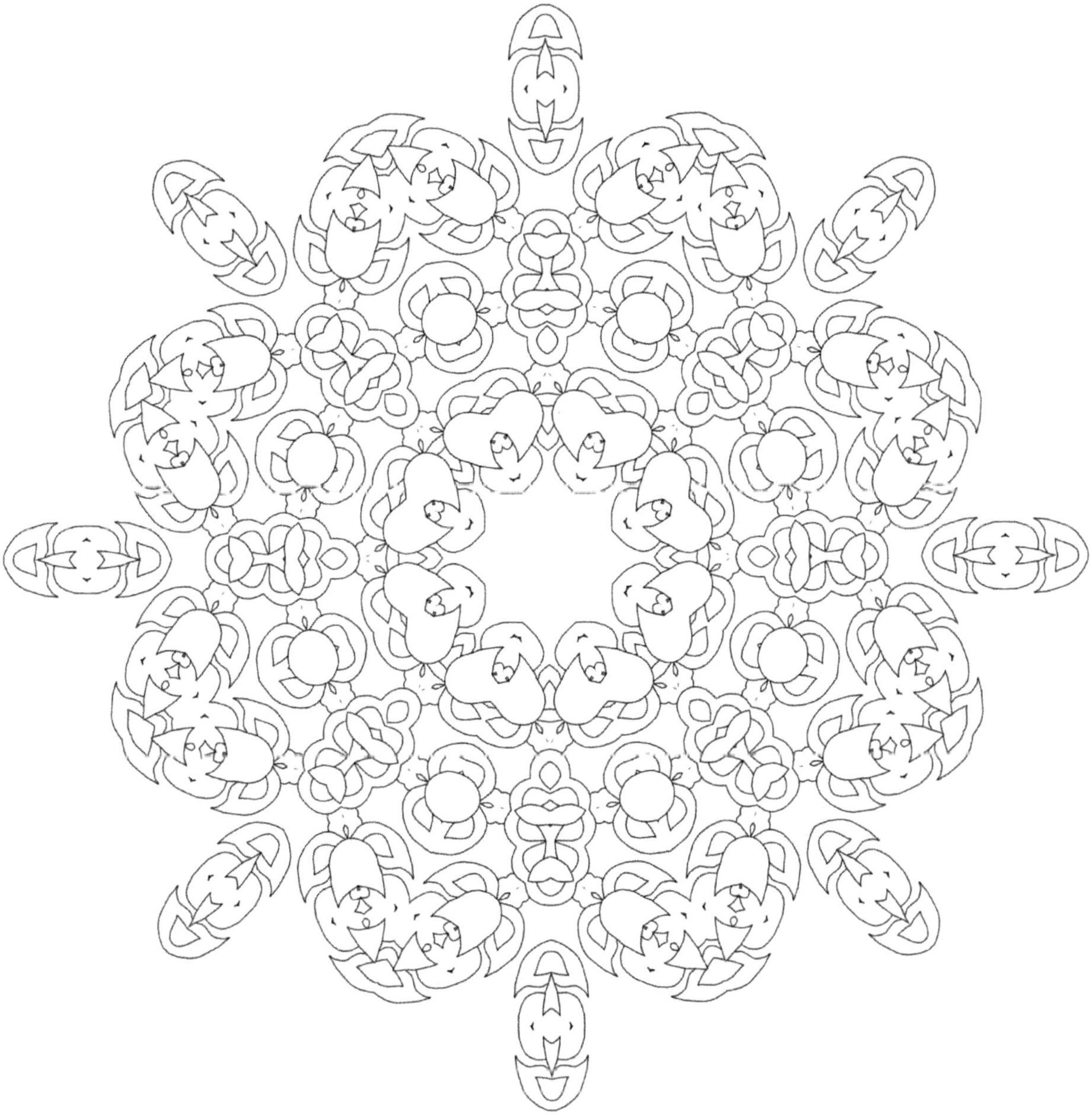

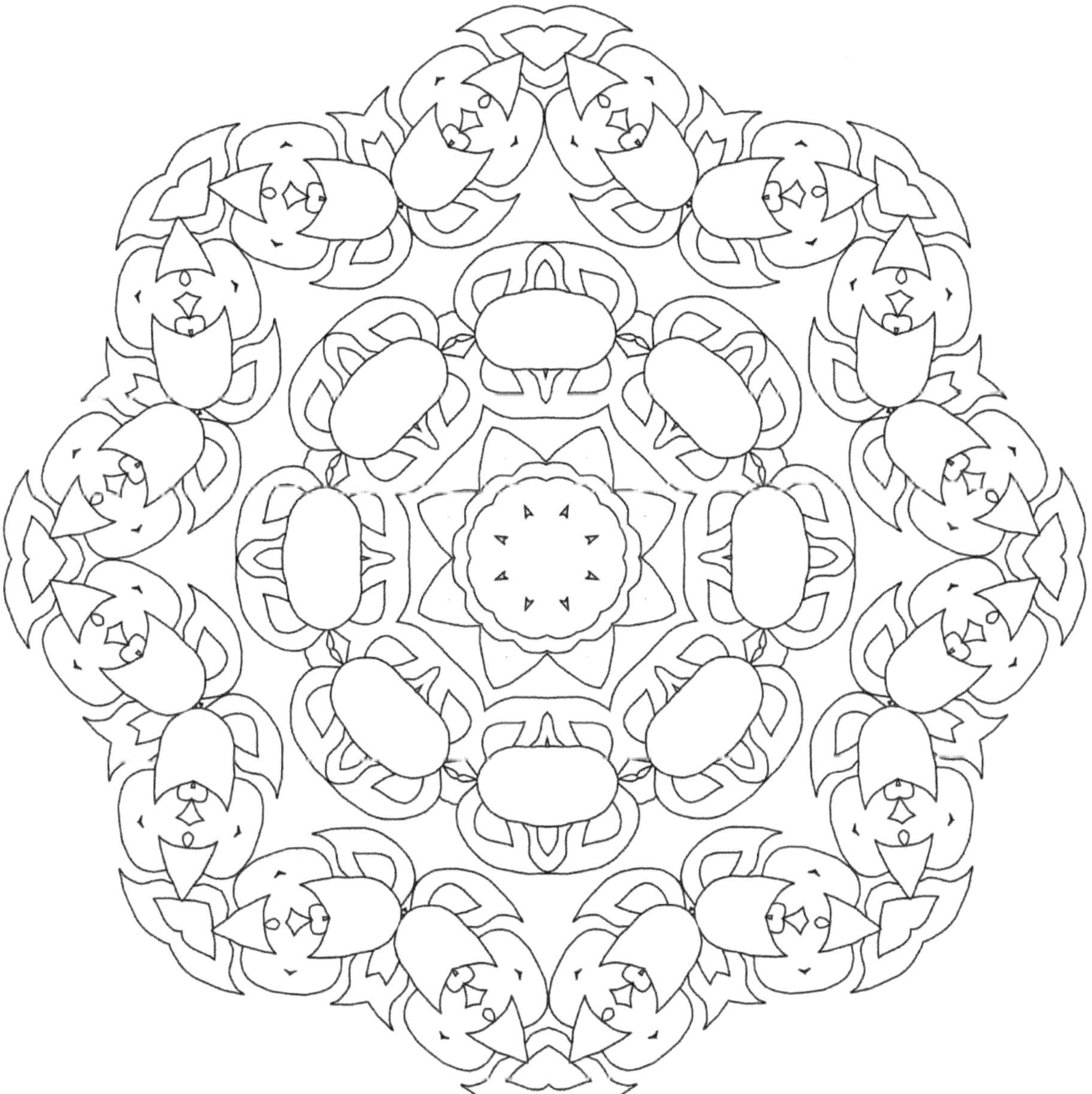

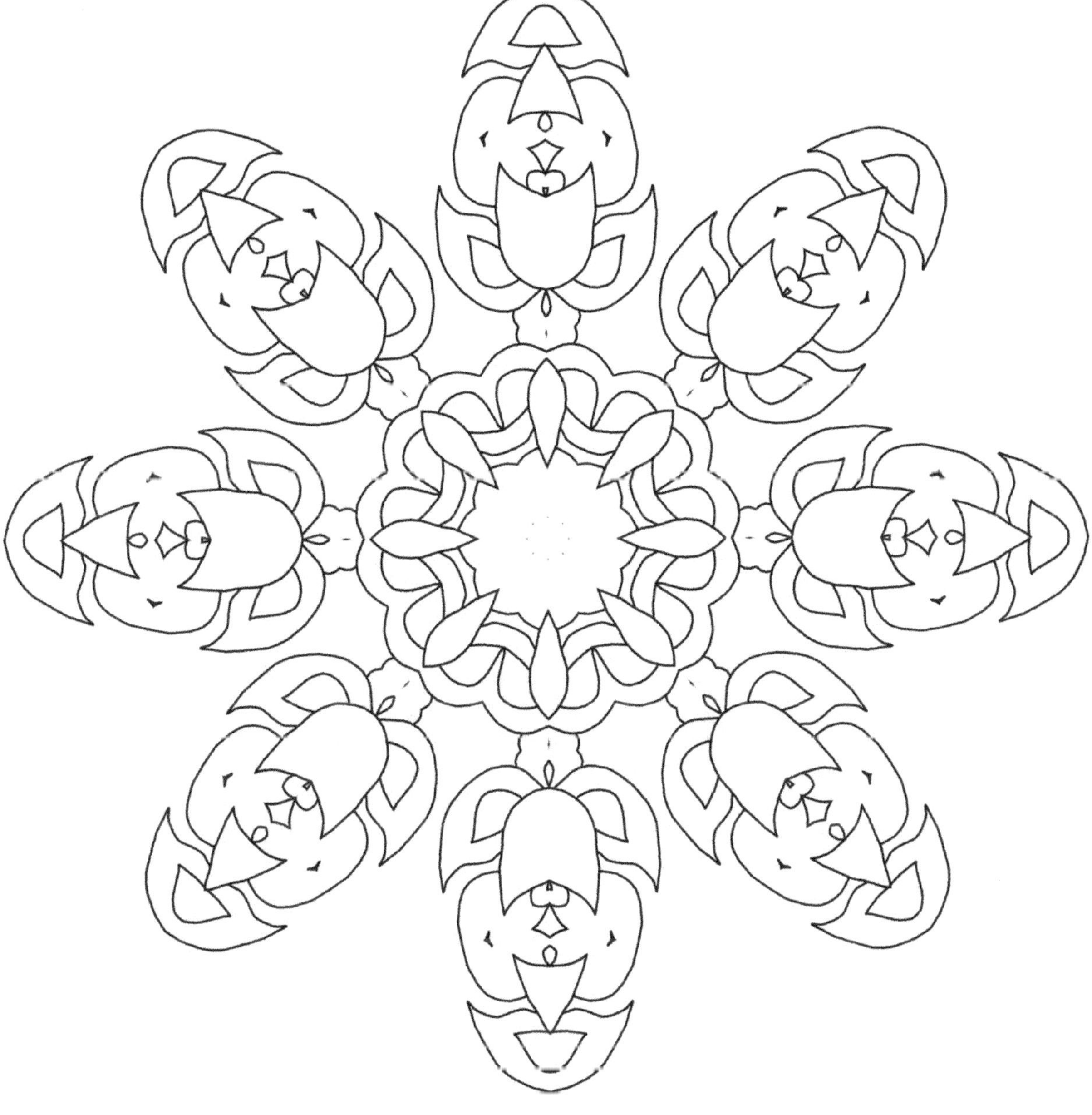

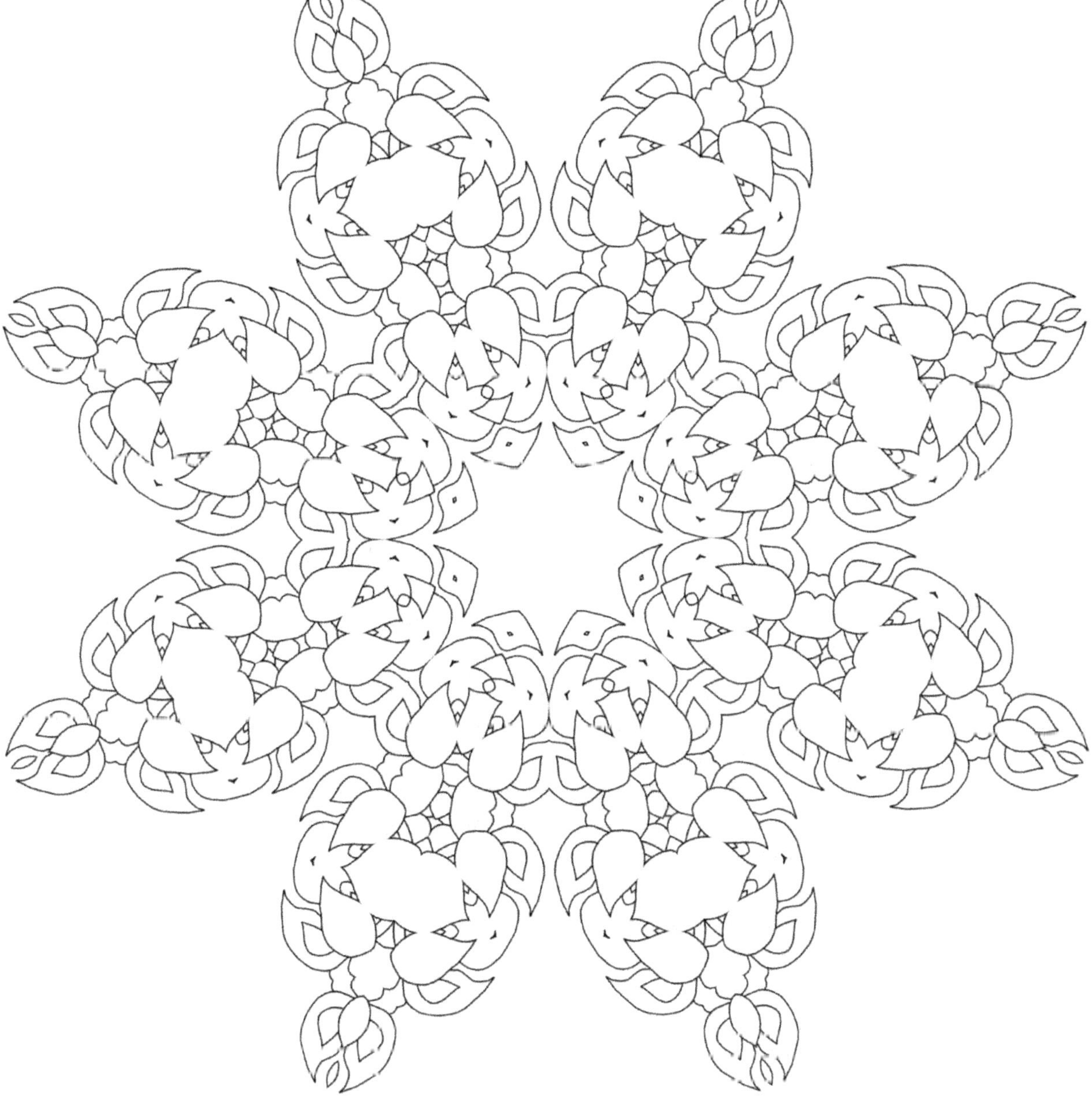

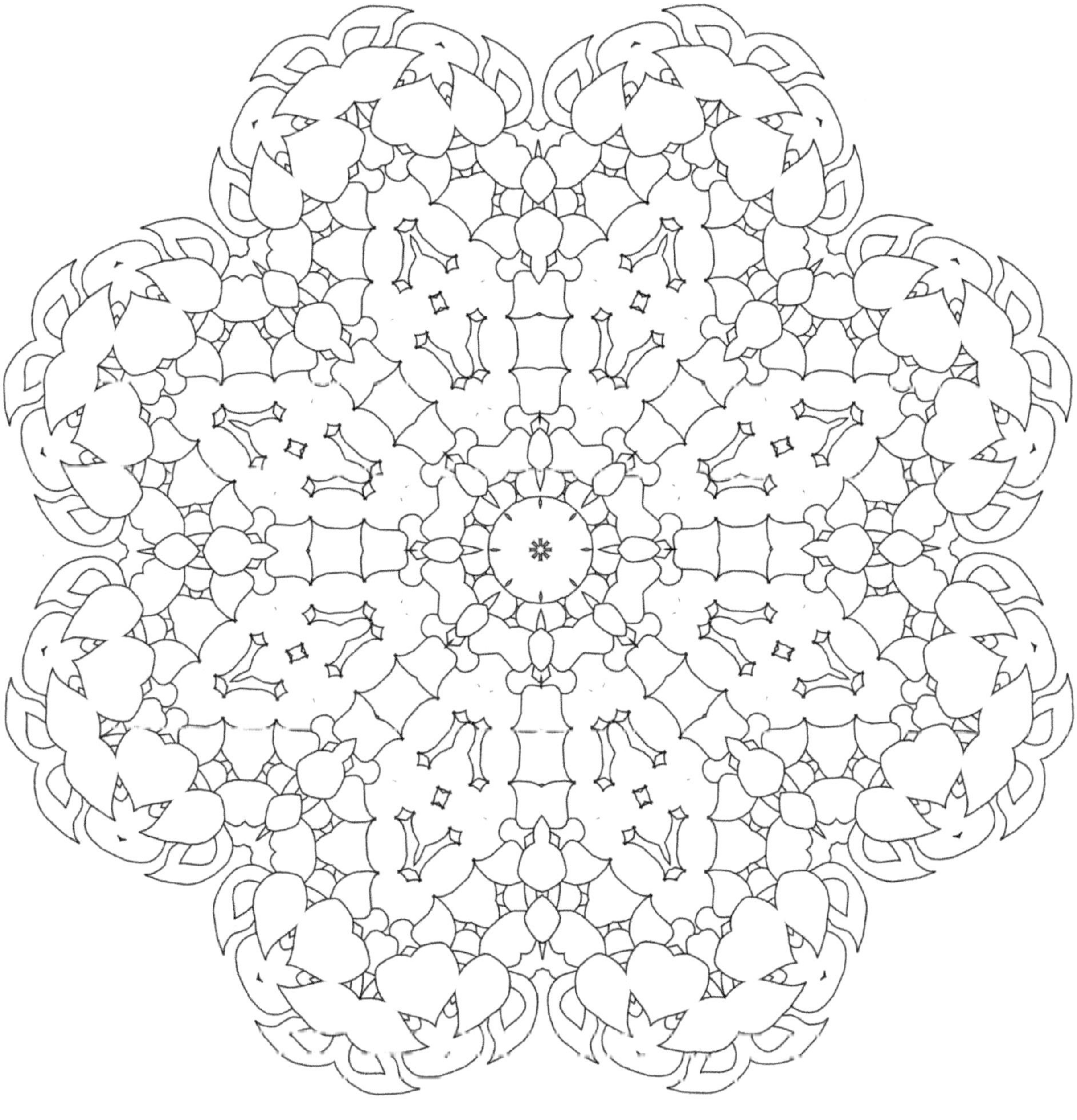

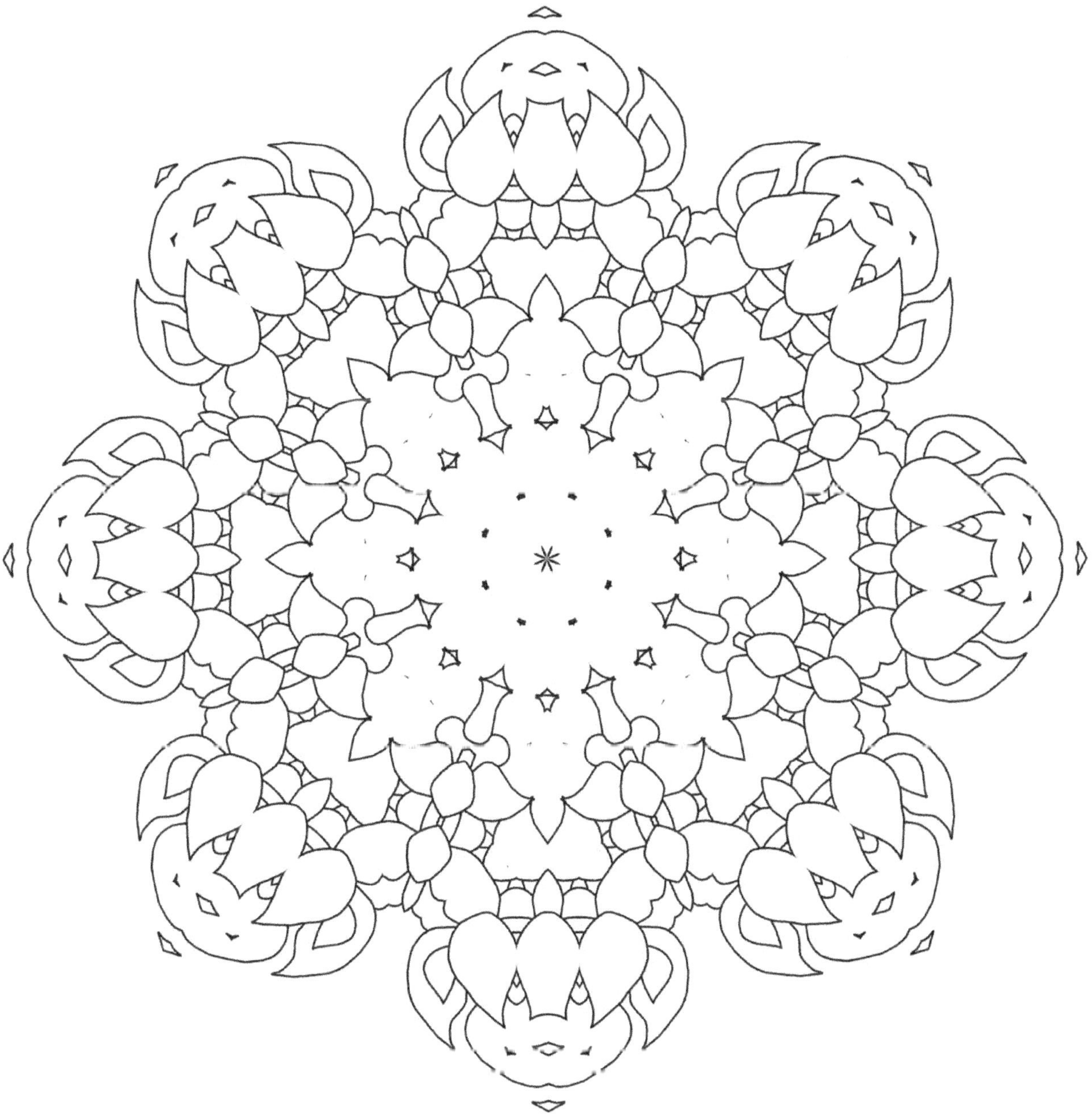

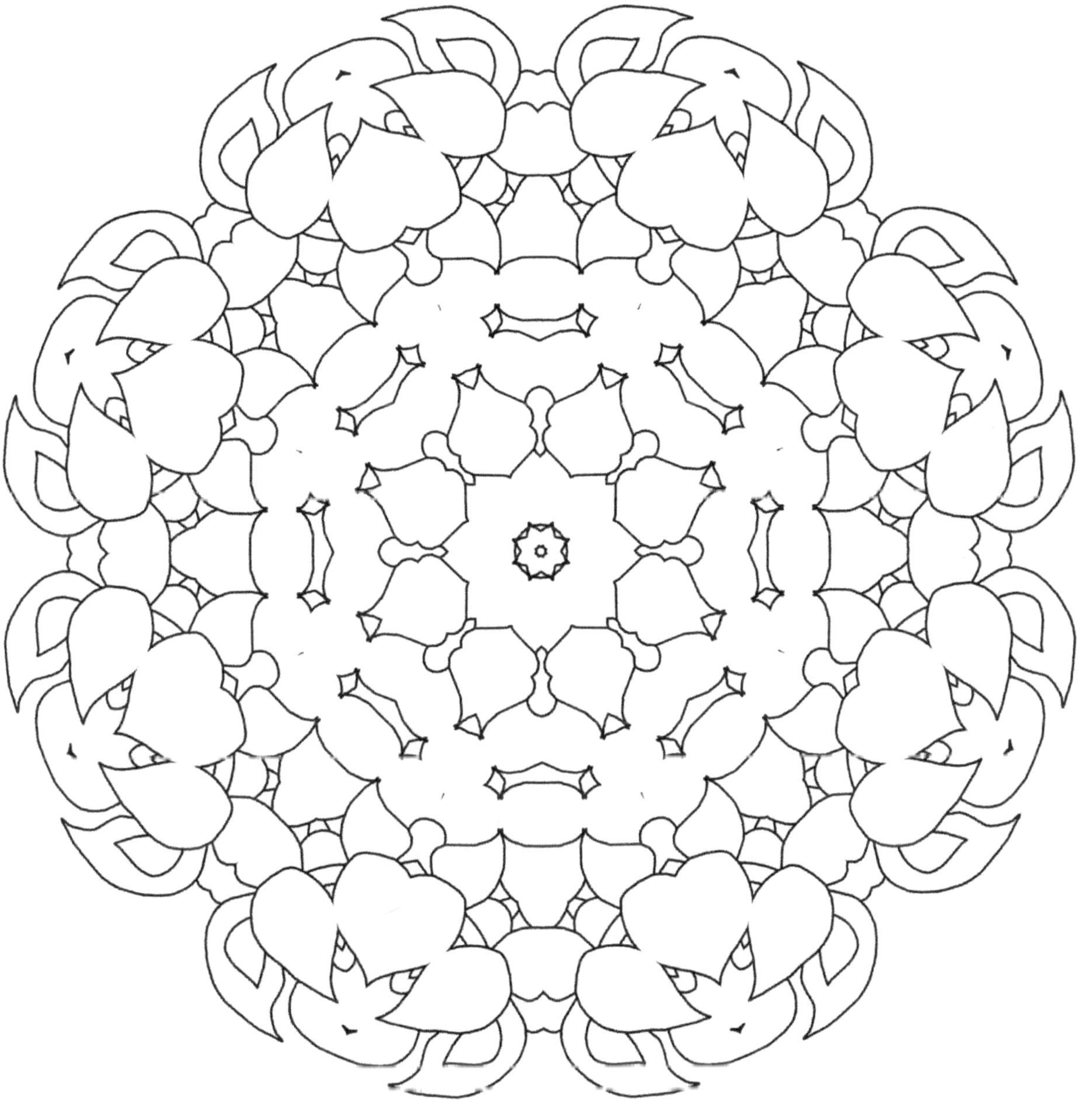

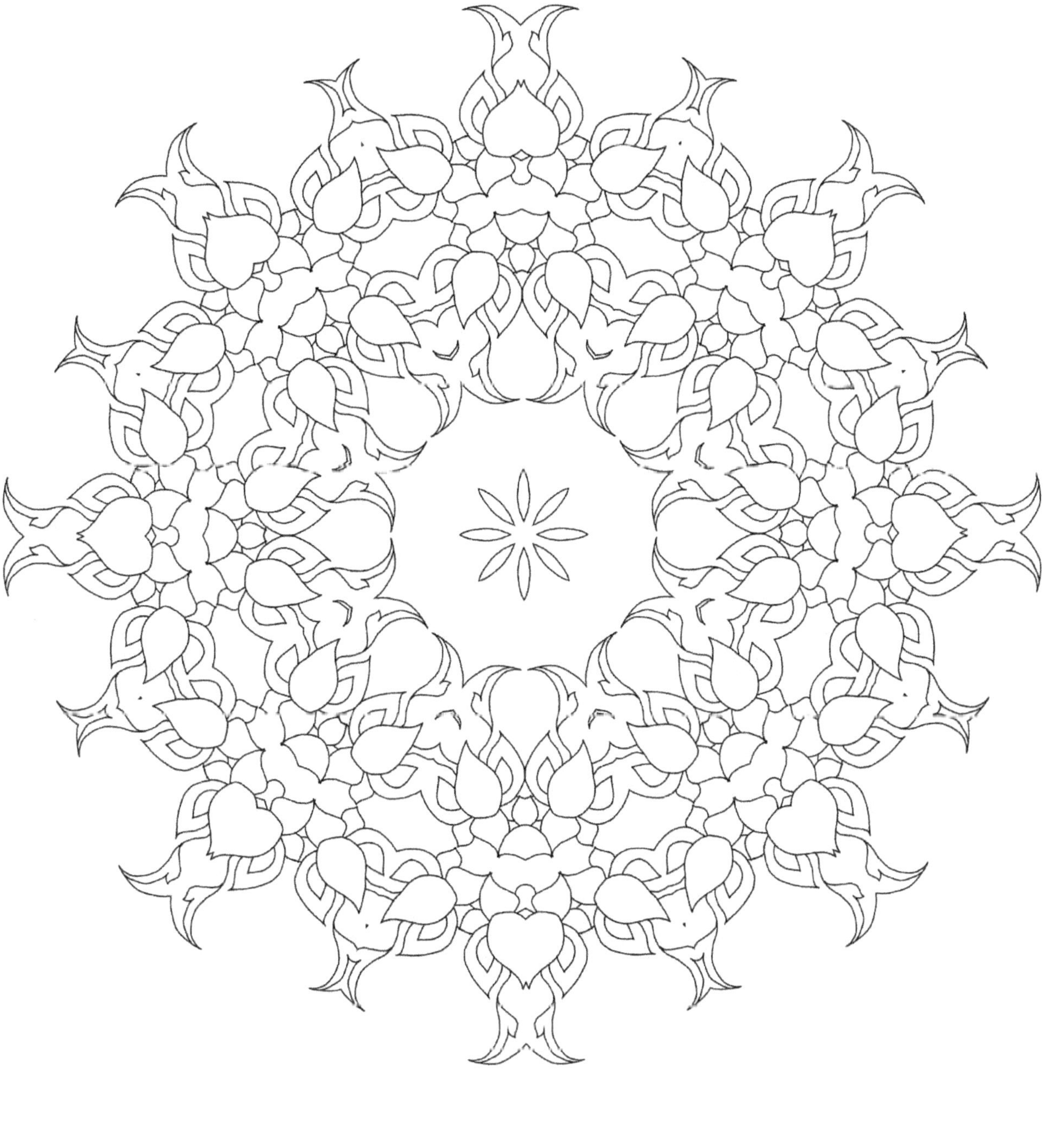

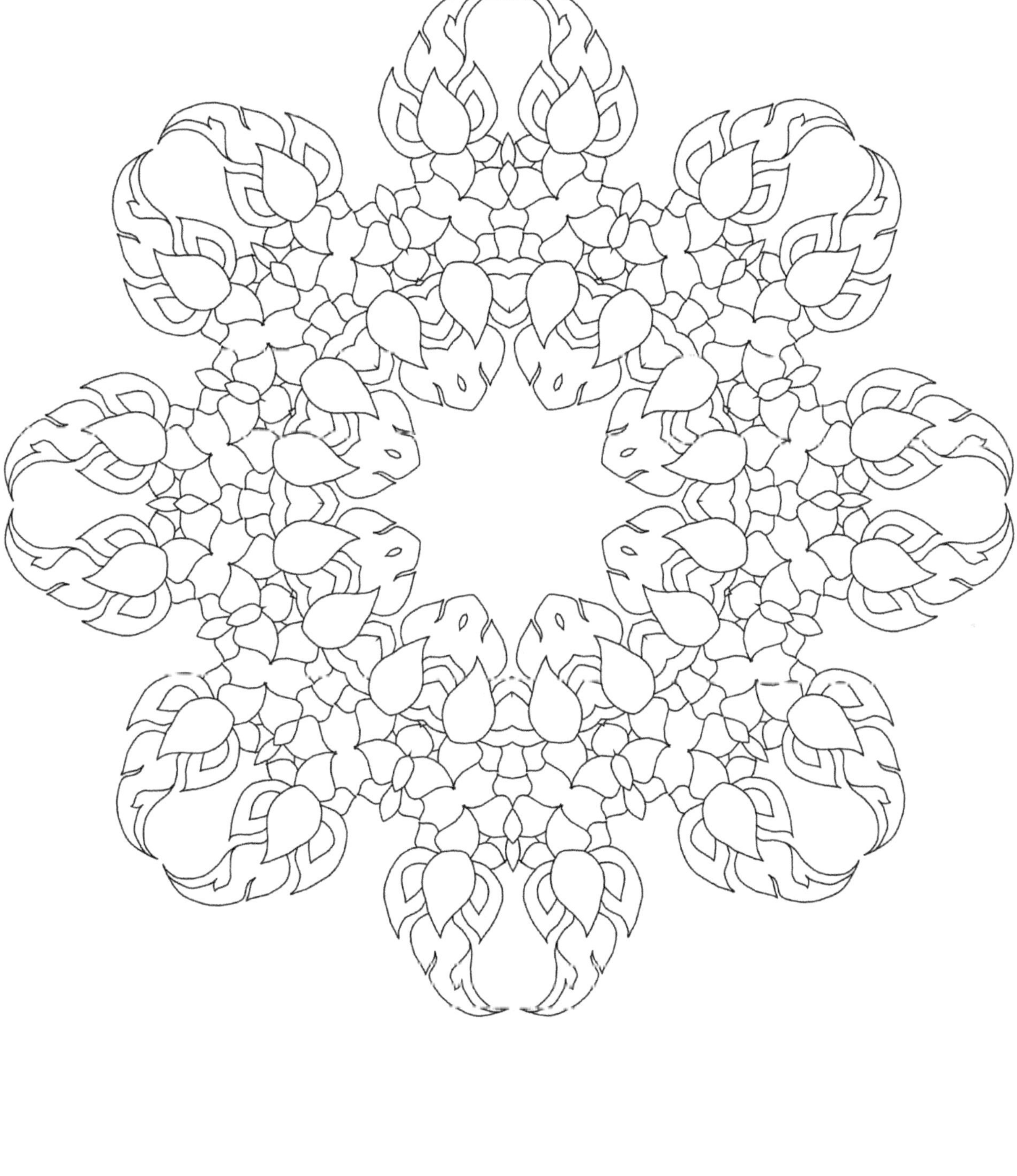

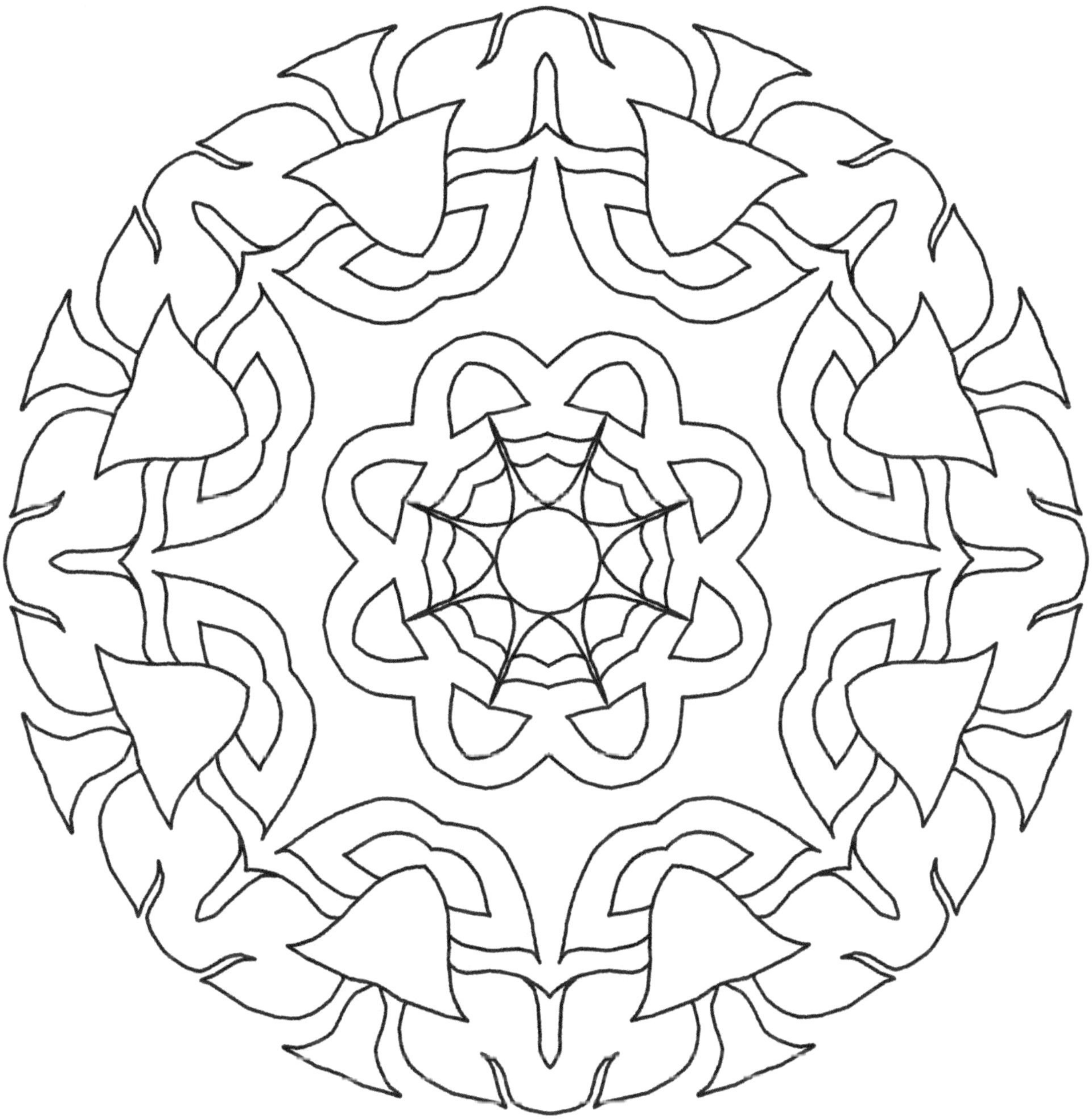

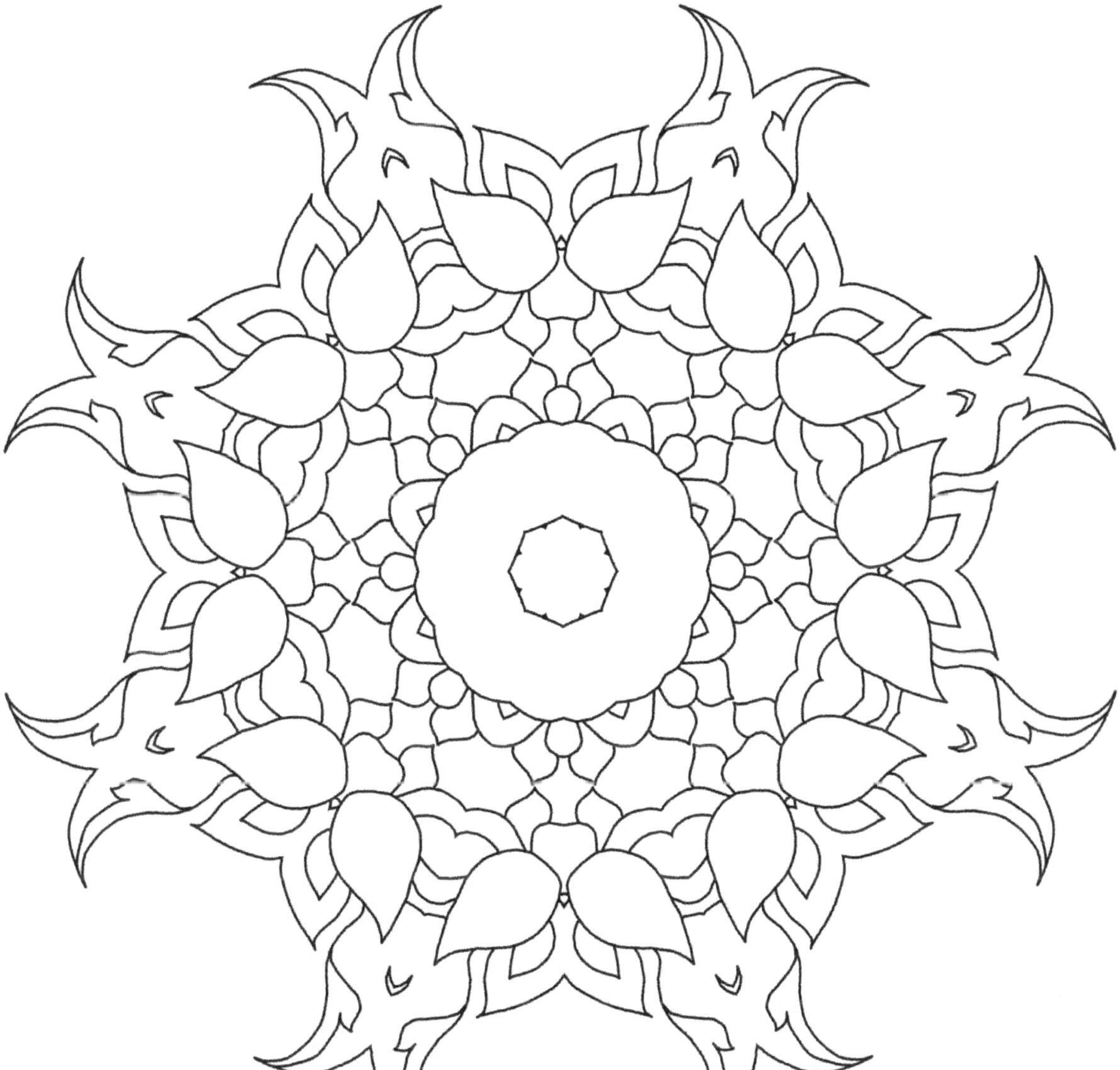

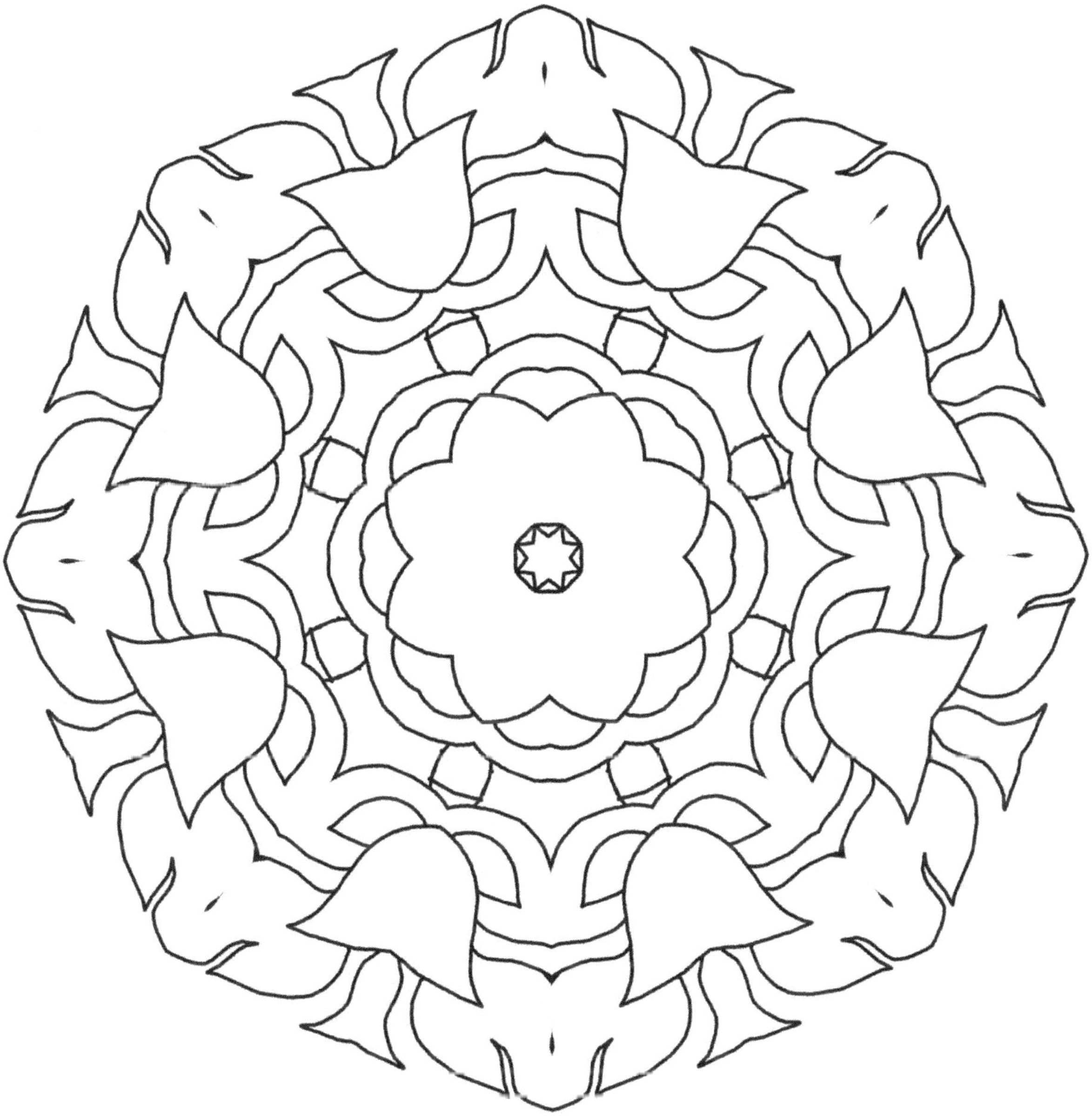

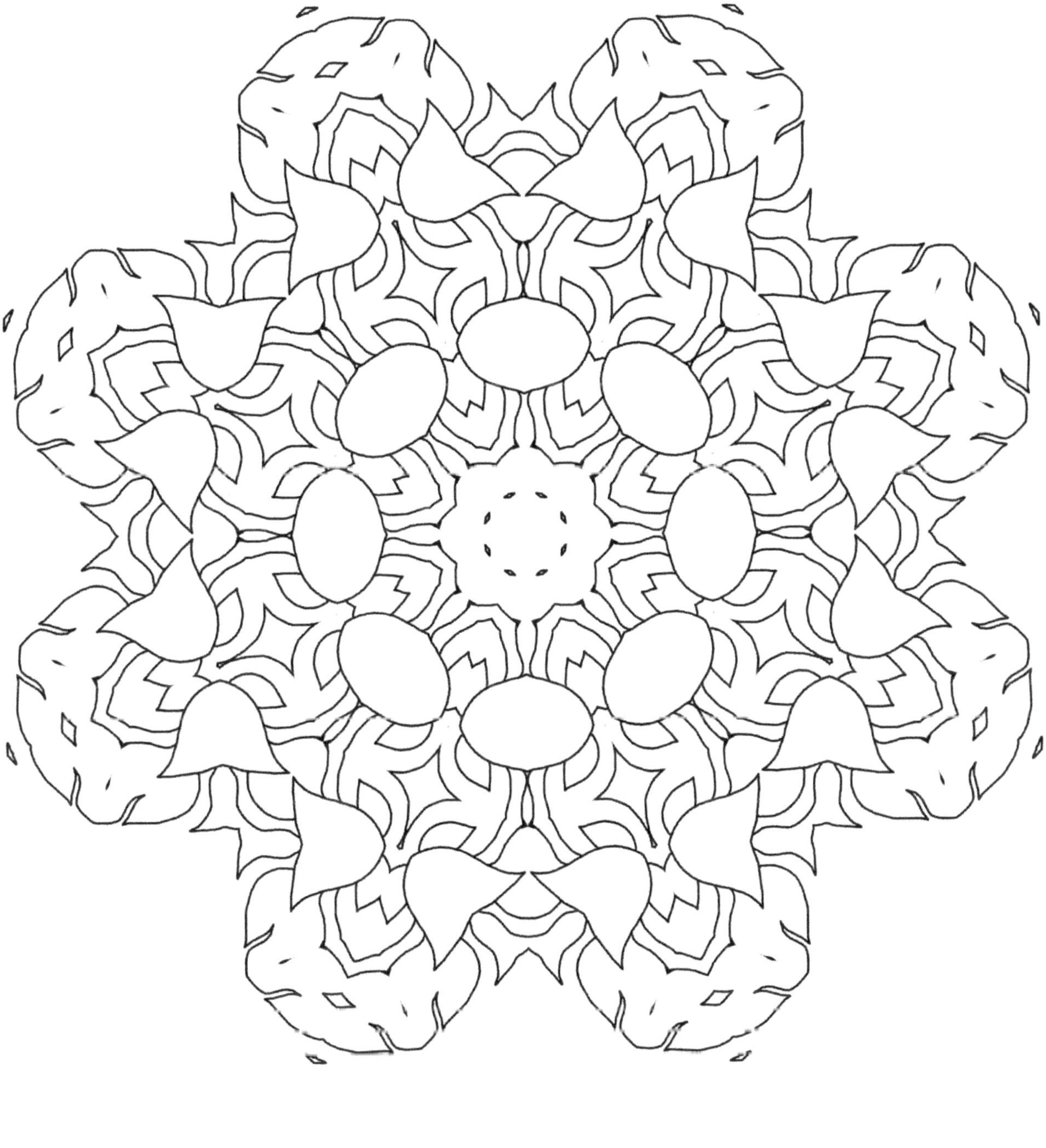

Thank you

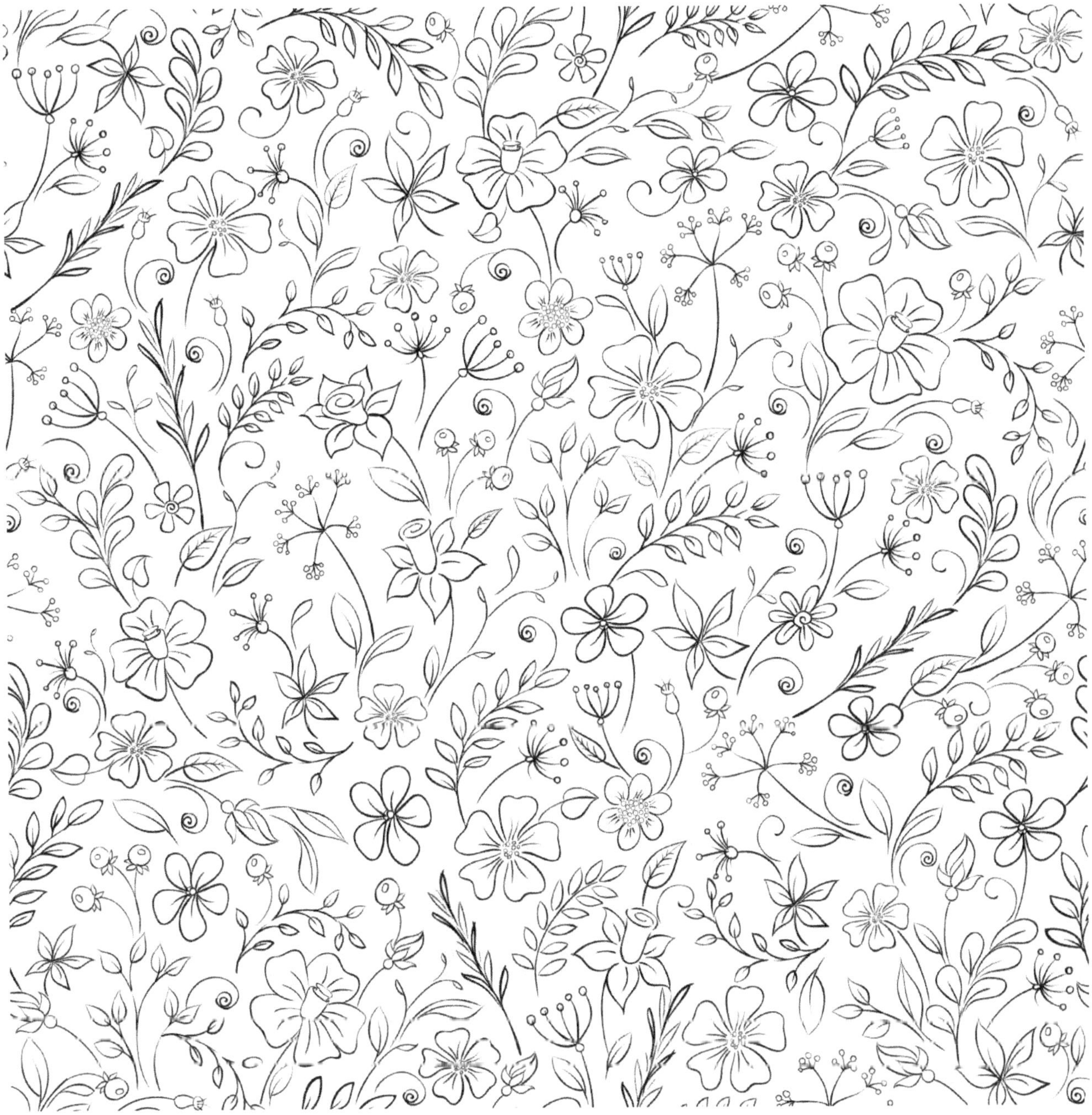

www.ingramcontent.com/pod-product-compliance
Lightning Source LLC
Chambersburg PA
CBHW081116180526
45170CB00008B/2862
* 9 7 8 1 5 4 2 6 7 9 9 0 9 *